EXPECT GREATER THINGS

FULFILLING YOUR GOD-GIVEN POTENTIAL AS A PERSON OF FAITH

DR. JOHN R. MYERS

COMMON THREAD MEDIA
Helping faith flourish.

FRANKLIN, TENNESSEE

Copyright 2008 John R. Myers

All Rights Reserved. No part of this book may be reproduced or transmitted in any form, or by any means, electronic or mechanical, including photocopying, recording or by any information storage and retrieval system, without permission in writing from the publisher.

Library of Congress Cataloging-in-Publication Data

Myers, John R., Dr.
Expect greater things: fulfilling your God-given potential as a person of faith / John R. Myers.
   p. cm.
  ISBN 978-1-934314-34-0 (alk. paper)
  1. Self-actualization (Psychology)--Religious aspects--Christianity.
2. Success--Religious aspects--Christianity. 3. Expectation--Religious aspects--Christianity. I. Title.

BV4598.2.M94 2008
248.4--dc22
                         2008007717

The following versions of the Bible are quoted in this work:
The Message: The Bible in Contemporary Language
New International Version
New King James Version
New Revised Standard Version.

Common Thread Media
101 Forrest Crossing Blvd., Ste. 100
Franklin, Tennessee 37064

Publisher: Dr. Douglas N. Norfleet
Production Editor: Kenneth L. Chumbley
Cover Design: Marc Pewitt

Printed in the United States of America
10 9 8 7 6 5 4 3 2 1

978-1-93431-434-0

Visit the Common Thread Media Web site at www.commonthreadmedia.com

This book is dedicated with love to my children

Stephanie Myers Perhach

and

Christopher Myers

May God continue to bless you as you

live life Expecting Greater Things!

With all my love,

Dad

CONTENTS

| FOREWORD | Dr. Robert H. Schuller | ix |

PART ONE
EXPECT GREATER THINGS

CHAPTER 1	Expect Greater Things	3
CHAPTER 2	Expect Greater Things Pioneers	9
CHAPTER 3	The Expect Greater Things Challenge	21
CHAPTER 4	Expect Greater Things Champions	31
CHAPTER 5	Greater Things Stoppers	41
CHAPTER 6	Expect Greater Things Launchers	55

PART TWO
GROW IN GREATER THINGS

CHAPTER 7	Grow in Greater Things Through the Disciplines of Prayer and Confession	65
CHAPTER 8	Grow in Greater Things Through the Spiritual Discipline of Study	74
CHAPTER 9	Three Key Areas to Grow in Greater Things	80
	Grow in Greater Things Spiritually	80
	Grow in Greater Things Relationally	87
	Grow in Greater Things Financially	92

PART THREE
DO GREATER THINGS

CHAPTER 10	Do Greater Things	99
CHAPTER 11	Do Greater Things through Generosity	105
CHAPTER 12	Do Greater Things for Your Community: Greater Things Champions	109
CHAPTER 13	Do Greater Things Environmentally	142
CHAPTER 14	Do Greater Things by Leaving a Lasting Legacy	157
CHAPTER 15	Expect, Grow, and Do Greater Things!	166
EPILOGUE		173

FOREWORD

Dr. John Myers brings to us the next generation of Possibility Thinking. It is called *Expect Greater Things*! I have known John for over a fifteen years and I can tell you that he is one of the dynamic leaders for the 21st Century. His vision and commitment to calling out the best in people for the good of all concerned is remarkable.

I first met John when he attended the second International School of Christian Communicators (ISOCC). He was one of twenty-five spiritual leaders who spent a week in the early 1990's at the Crystal Cathedral ISOCC studying how to effectively and holistically communicate the message of God's love.

John and I also served together on the General Council of Churches Uniting in Global Ministries (CUGM) for several years. We also worked together to impact postcommunist Russia through the Russian Farm Project, as well as other endeavors that teach values, ethics, spirituality, solid business practices, and the power of faith.

It has been great to watch John grow in his faith. His perspective on the significance of the power of positive thinking and the significance of possibility thinking has deepened substantially through the years. Through this growth and maturing process, John now brings to us a natural extension of the power of positive Christianity and theology: *Expect Greater Things*. In fact, the first time that John and I discussed Greater Things was at a CUGM conference in Phoenix, Arizona at the Community Church of Joy. He shared with me that it was based on Jesus' words in John 14:12-14. You will see this in the first chapter of the book. I told him that the concept was excellent and that this was John's further calling from God. And, I still believe it today.

John's Greater Things principles for living will inspire you to Expect Greater Things, Grow in Greater Things, and Do Greater Things spiritually, relationally, financially, physically, nutritionally, recreationally, environmentally, and philanthropically. John gives you practical handles for applying the themes of each chapter through his Greater Things "Points to Ponder" and Greater Things "Questions for Reflection".

This book, the first of several in the *Expect Greater Things* line, will challenge, inspire, and motivate you. In *Expect Greater Things* you will learn how to fulfill your God-given potential as a person of faith. John will guide you through his personal stories and experiences, knowledge of the Bible, scholars of old, as well as contemporary authors and leaders. You will travel with him on adventures of faith, struggle, success, and accomplishment. Your life will be enriched through these stories and the truths that he has gleaned. And, if you choose, your life can be enhanced and even changed. His keynotes, writing, and seminars will challenge, inspire, and motivate you to make a difference.

In addition, John introduces you to Greater Things "Pioneers" and Greater Things "Champions." These stories of faith-filled people will motivate you to Expect, Grow, and Do Greater Things!

When you complete *Expect Greater Things*, you will have an understanding both in your heart and your mind of God's love for you and the tremendous potential that you have for living your life to the fullest!

May God bless you as you read *Expect Greater Things*! All I can say is "Wow!"

Dr. Robert H. Schuller
Founding Pastor, The Crystal Cathedral
January 13, 2008

PART ONE

EXPECT GREATER THINGS

CHAPTER 1
EXPECT GREATER THINGS

Tommy loved playing baseball. At the age of eight he was fully engaged in Little League. In fact, each day Tommy arrived thirty minutes before baseball practice and worked on a different part of his game.

One day, Tommy was out on the field practicing his game. He tossed the ball up! He swung. He missed. He tossed the ball up! He swung. He missed. Again, He tossed the ball up! He swung. He missed. This continued for twenty minutes.

His coach, who had arrived and witnessed the excruciating process, couldn't believe it. He approached Tommy with strength and sensitivity. He said, "Tommy, I can help you! It is all about eye–hand coordination. You toss the ball up . . . keep your eye on the ball . . . and swing! You will definitely hit it and improve your batting."

"Improve my batting?" Tommy replied. "Hey, I am practicing my pitching!"

Tommy knew what he wanted! He expected greater things of himself and his game. He knew the secrets to living effectively. Vision! Focus! Practice! More than likely, Tommy grew up to be an excellent all-star pitcher!

The application of Vision, Focus, and Practice is that which births a Greater Things' lifestyle.

<u>Expect</u> Greater Things
<u>Grow in</u> Greater Things
<u>Do</u> Greater Things
These three phrases can change your life!

Do you expect greater things in your life? Do you want to grow in greater things? Do you want to have a passion that compels you to do greater things with your life to impact others positively? Then, Expect! Grow! Do! These are the keys to living a fulfilled, happy, and positively challenging life. That is what this book and subsequent books in this Expect Greater Things series are all about! It is also what www.expectgreaterthings.com creates: a one stop shop for significance and the greater things journey for your life!

In fact, the sequel to this foundational book will be *Expect Greater Things: Twelve Principles for Excellence in Living*.

Where did this lifestyle philosophy and belief system develop? I have always loved to read the classics, study ancient history and thought, as well as read the Bible and contemporary authors of psychology, theology, business, investing, wealth management, philanthropy, and leadership. In addition, my life has been blessed with great opportunities to travel the world. To date, I have traveled to twenty-eight countries and much of the United States. Each time I travel to another country, I make it a habit to read and study the history, culture, sociology, politics, economics, belief systems, and people of the country to which I am traveling. This prepares me for a full experience that is deep and meaningful. It is like enjoying a five-course meal at a top restaurant . . . all of the flavors exude with excellent service and meal preparation.

The opposite experience would be to simply hop on a jet and travel to the destination without preparation. All you would experience this way are the superficial *tourist traps* and a cursory glance at life in the country you are visiting. This is like going to a fast food drive through and ordering a meal that is fast, greasy, and filling. As soon as you get the meal, you take it out of the bag and wolf it down before your next meeting or activity. In fact, if someone asked what you ate for lunch that day, you would probably not even remember . . . unless you are suffering from indigestion.

Life is either a five course meal or a fast food fury. We can either Expect Greater Things and enjoy the journey to the fullest, or we can expect the status quo and skip through life by going to all the superficial tourist traps without ever truly understanding why we are here.

The tourist trap lifestyle of superficiality can get ingrained in our habit of *going through the motions*. This is the path of least resistance that results in a person living a life of quiet desperation, having learned to be content with the status quo.

The results are lots of nice people who go through the daily grind, only to wake up the next morning to go through it again. They open the morning paper and read the obituary pages. If their name isn't on it, they get showered, dressed, and set out for another day of tourist trap and status quo living. Instead of accomplishing something really fantastic with their life's force, they exist *primarily* to exist. They serve themselves beautifully. In fact, they might even have achieved the American dream with the house, family, friends, cars, club memberships, and all the other trappings. But at the end of the day there is a nagging question: isn't there more to life? Besides accumulating, shouldn't there be some giving beyond the self, or one's family, or circle of influence? It reminds me of the old Peggy Lee song that asks, "Is That All There Is?"

In fact, when an opportunity comes to be of service to someone outside the circle, the energy and the resources to accomplish a greater thing is often not there. No one benefits except those who are already at the core.

Think about it! An individual who spends all of their energy simply getting by will not reach out beyond themselves because it will upset their status quo. The same is true with an organization or business. Phrases, such as, "we've never done it that way," or "I tried that once and it didn't work out," or "what will others think?" or "let's not rock the boat," become the mantras of life. And the more we repeat something, the more it becomes our reality. Wow!—what a sad way to live life!

I lived that lifestyle through my midteens. I was brought up in a great family. We had a nice home, golf course memberships, a lake house, a couple of boats, good friends, and family. It was really a great life. I grew up the youngest of five children. We had lots of aunts and uncles and cousins. It wasn't unusual to have fifty people at our home for Christmas and New Years Eve parties. It was so much fun! One of my fondest memories was that of Christmas caroling. We caroled in the cold Indiana weather from the time I was five years old until I was twenty-one. We went to friend's homes, shut-in relatives' homes, and always ended the evening at our family's home with more singing, hot chocolate, and all kinds of Christmas goodies. It was amazing. I was learning the power of family and community . . . the power of belonging, happiness, identity, and purpose. But even with this amazing gift, there was a nagging question in my heart: "is that all there is?"

My father was an outstanding businessman. He owned several restaurants in our hometown of Marion, Indiana. He provided well for our family and helped shape the lives of many people who were in his employ.

One of my earliest childhood memories is that of being with my Mom, Dad, brothers, and sisters at our small lake cottage located at Secrist Lake in northern Indiana. It had a wonderful picture window that looked over the lake.

As a little child I would sit on my father's lap at night and look across the lake through the picture window. We would see the lights of the other cottages, and make up stories about the people who lived there. Other times we would watch headlights dance across the water toward our shore. Each dancing headlight stirred our imaginations, and we devised tales of meetings with the drivers from the distant shore. The shore might as well have been the other side of the world to a little boy of five.

The night lights helped develop a feeling of community around that small Indiana lake. Even more importantly, my father and I shared a common message and story. This gave me security and an inner desire to reach out across the lake and make the feeling of community more than a feeling—I wanted to make it a reality.

The way I went about creating a community at the lake was on the water. As a young boy, teenager, and even young adult, I would drive our boat around the shore and greet people warmly. They would exchange the greeting. Sometimes we would stop our boats, link up, and talk. Often, great friendships were developed. Soon the lights in the houses represented real names, faces, and stories behind their glow. No longer was our lake an imaginary community; it was a community.

There are many other wonderful stories about my growing up years. I truly had a great time and was blessed with a great family and friends. And yet, with all of the abundance and all of those great blessings, I felt as if something was missing.

So, at about the age of sixteen I started asking the age-old questions: Who am I? Why am I here? What's the purpose of life? Is there a God? If so, how can I believe in Him and what does it take? I didn't know it then, but this was the beginning of a lifelong quest that would teach me to Expect Greater Things, Grow in Greater Things, and Do Greater Things. And, the journey has been amazing! I will tell you that the journey has not always been easy, but no journey is always easy. It is, however, tremendously adventuresome and fulfilling!

God wants us to achieve our fullest potential by cultivating the richness of the human spirit combined with the awesomeness of faith. When we live life in this manner, we are amazed at the greater things that happen! In fact, we discover that the more we live with this frame of mind, the more greater things actually happen! And, not only do they happen to us personally, but greater things occur in every phase of our lives with a ripple effect that touches and affects others! We thus come to live a life of meaning, not meaninglessness. It is a life of abundance, positive surprises, unbelievable connectivity with God and others, and tremendous influence. This is the Expect Greater Things lifestyle.

I have personally experienced this lifestyle for most of my life and I can vouch for living with a greater things mindset. I will share my personal experiences and observations throughout this book as to the phenomenal effects that result from living with a greater things point of view, lifestyle, discipline, and practice. I experience the greater things lifestyle on three distinct levels: I expect greater things (Part One), I expect to grow in greater things (Part Two), and I expect to do greater things (Part Three). My life's study and practice teach me that in order to experience a jam-packed greater things lifestyle; one must first begin with Expecting Greater Things!

But how is that done? Well, just as when I prepare for a trip to a foreign country I research the history and beginnings of that country, Expecting Greater Things can similarly be viewed as a country of thought, practice, and powerfully positive results that can be researched and studied. It has its roots in the Bible and many ancient books of wisdom, and draws on contemporary thinkers of the twentieth and twenty-first centuries.

POINTS TO PONDER

- Life can be a wonderful journey filled with dynamic purpose, or it can be filled with superficial tourist trappings which maintain the status quo
- Life is either a five-course meal, or a fast-food fury.
- God wants us to achieve our fullest potential by cultivating the richness of the human spirit, combined with the awesomeness of faith.

QUESTIONS FOR REFLECTION

- Do I expect greater things in my life? Do I want to grow in greater things? Do I want to have a passion that compels me to do greater things with my life?
- Do I view my life as a first-class trip or a tourist-trap experience?
- Am I enjoying the fullness of a five-course dining experience or am I into the fast-food fury of the status quo?

When the student is ready, the teacher appears!

CHAPTER 2

EXPECT GREATER THINGS PIONEERS

I will never forget the day when I was leading a study of the New Testament book of St. John, one of the four Gospels (Matthew, Mark, Luke, and John), which tell of the life and times of Jesus. It was a cold, snowy night in northern Indiana at the church I served in South Bend. The year was 1997. I was leading an evening Bible study with about thirty people in attendance. I was teaching about the love that Jesus had shown those who loved him as he was preparing them for his death on the cross. I read a passage that I had read many times before, but that night it had an amazing impact on my thinking and perception. It was as if the words jumped off the page into my heart and mind. There is a saying that when the student is ready, the teacher appears. All I can tell you is this: at the age of forty, the student must have been ready—because the teacher showed up and changed my life that night and the day to follow. The text was John 14:12–14 where Jesus said, "You will do greater things than these because I go to the Father."

It was then that I began to understand how personal experience, sound thinking, and the power of faith combined to make an amazing difference not only in my life, but also in the lives of other people, in dynamic and powerful ways! Wow!

The next morning, February 20, 1997, while I was looking out the window of my study at home, which overlooked our frozen lake,

I read that text again. And like a download from a Web site, I got a full vision of Expecting Greater Things, Growing in Greater Things, and Doing Greater Things, as well as the blueprint that is the Web site for Greater Things Enterprises, LLC: www.expectgreaterthings.com. And now, finally, you can benefit from this download, which occurred over one decade ago!

The lesson here is this: you can expect greater things and find a great vision and dream for something larger than your life. And if it energizes and benefits you, builds others up, and results in a systemic change in the lives of the larger community, then it is a Greater Things opportunity. But it might not happen overnight; in fact, it might take a long time.

I have been nurturing my dream and vision of Greater Things for over a decade, but I never stopped believing that God had planted this vision in my life and heart so that I could help impact your life as mine has been impacted. Greater Things have been happening in and through my life since I was a child, but I didn't put my finger on what it was until I discovered the power of Expecting, Growing in, and Doing Greater Things.

Over the years our world has been fortunate to have known some wonderful "Expect Greater Things" pioneers who have helped to shape faith, culture, and the inner self with their philosophies and teachings. Most recently, we can look to the twentieth century and the early twenty-first century to find some like-minded thinkers who influenced millions of people with their inspirational outlook on life.

The latter half of the twentieth century ushered in the first generation of expecting greater things thinking with the philosophies, psychological theories, and theologies of such noted leaders as Fulton J. Sheen, Norman Vincent Peale, Robert Schuller, Billy Graham, Carl Rogers, and Napoleon Hill, to name just a few. Each one, in his own way, emphasized the significance of using the mind, body, and spirit to position one's energy, faith, hope, love, and influence for the purpose of focusing on the positive possibilities of a full and abundant life. These great leaders, thinkers, visionaries, and speakers compelled their audience and readers to think outside the box in order to realize their full potential.

The four pastors on the list—Bishop Fulton J. Sheen, Dr. Billy Graham, Dr. Norman Vincent Peale, and Dr. Robert H. Schuller—were pioneers who helped make faith in God and the self accessible and understandable. They downplayed the negative and accentuated the positive. Each of these leaders helped people in every walk of life understand that with God's love and compassion, combined with faith in both God and oneself, all things are possible. Each one gave people hope without browbeating them with legalism. Each one offered the gospel of God's love through Jesus Christ in pragmatic ways that made Christianity a practical, experiential, and commonsense faith. And each used his writings and the power of the mass media to reach millions of people. Some of the people these pioneers reached belonged to churches, but many did not. Some had fallen away from God, and these pioneers helped them come back to a faith relationship with God.

A case in point was my own family. When I was five years old, our family quit attending the United Methodist Church in my hometown of Marion, Indiana. My father owned five restaurants and he kept them open on Sundays. The year was 1962, and we were in the Bible Belt. One Sunday morning during church service, the pastor declared from the pulpit that it was wrong to keep a business open on Sundays. He looked straight at my father. Well, Dad was a pretty easygoing fellow. He decided to take it in stride and not let it bother him. That was until later that same Sunday afternoon, when my father and mother were at the local Kroger store buying groceries. Who do you think that they saw? Sure enough, the pastor from First United Methodist Church. The incongruity between the minister's Sunday morning message and his Sunday afternoon activities really upset my father, and, basically, our family stopped attending traditional church service on Sunday mornings for several years.

It was Dr. Robert H. Schuller's message of possibility thinking and Norman Vincent Peale's message of the power of positive thinking that reignited the faith in my parents some thirteen years later. I remember vividly in the mid-1970s seeing Norman Vincent Peale's *Guidepost* magazine on the coffee table in our family room. And each Sunday morning, *The Hour of Power* with Dr. Robert H. Schuller would grace our family room television set. My mother and father both commented on how the positive influence of these two pastors' messages brought them back to a faith relationship with God. Both of these leaders had a tremendous influence in shaping our family's faith development. Their emphasis was not on what you can't do if you are a religious person, but rather on what you can do if you are a person of faith. There is a huge difference between being religious and being faithful.

All four pastors made significant contributions to what I have coined Expecting Greater Things.

Bishop Fulton J. Sheen promoted a practical, hard-hitting faith in God that met life head on. Bishop Sheen's renowned television series, *Life Is Worth Living*, was watched by millions. His timeless insights offered wise, personal, and inspiring guidance on the problems affecting our lives in today's world. Bishop Sheen encouraged millions to expect greater things in life through their faith in God and each other.

Dr. Billy Graham, perhaps the greatest evangelist of the twentieth century, presented the gospel of God's love through Jesus Christ in no-nonsense, direct messages that appealed to stadiums full of people, as well as national audiences who were riveted to their televisions. Dr. Graham's organization still thrives on helping people discover their faith and a relationship with God. The message is simple:

- God is love.
  - We are all in need of a Savior.
  - That Savior is Jesus Christ.
  - Turn your life around by confessing:
    That you are a sinner in need of forgiveness.
    That you wish to invite Jesus Christ to be your Savior and Lord.
    That you will do so now by praying for Jesus Christ to come into your life forever.
  - Find a person you know and tell him or her of your decision.

- Start attending a local church in your community where you can grow your faith and understand more fully the decision you have made.

Dr. Graham inspired millions of people to make a decision to come to faith in his world-famous crusades. I remember watching the television with awe as hundreds and sometimes thousands of people would leave their seats in the stadium to go down front to pray to receive Christ in their hearts. Amazing! The song would always be the same, "Just As I Am":

JUST AS I AM

Just as I am, without one plea, but that Thy blood was shed for me,
And that Thou bidst me come to Thee, O Lamb of God, I come, I come.

Just as I am, and waiting not to rid my soul of one dark blot,
To Thee whose blood can cleanse each spot, O Lamb of God, I come, I come.

Just as I am, though tossed about with many a conflict, many a doubt,
Fightings and fears within, without, O Lamb of God, I come, I come.

Just as I am, poor, wretched, blind; sight, riches, healing of the mind,
Yea, all I need in Thee to find, O Lamb of God, I come, I come.

Just as I am, Thou wilt receive, Wilt welcome, pardon, cleanse, relieve;
Because Thy promise I believe, O Lamb of God, I come, I come.

Just as I am, Thy love unknown hath broken every barrier down;
Now, to be Thine, yea, Thine alone, O Lamb of God, I come, I come.

The history behind this well-known hymn is an Expect Greater Things story in and of itself. Miss Charlotte Elliott was visiting some friends in the West End of London, and there she met the eminent minister César Malan. While they were seated at supper, the minister said he hoped that she was a Christian. She took offense at this, and replied that she would rather not discuss that question. Dr. Malan said that he was sorry if he had offended her, that he always liked to speak a word for his Master, and that he hoped that the young lady would someday become a worker for Christ. When they met again, at the home of a mutual friend three weeks later, Miss Elliott told the minister that ever since he had spoken to her she had been trying to find her Savior, and that she now wished him to tell her how to come to Christ. "Just come to him as you are," Dr. Malan said. This she did, and she went away rejoicing. Shortly afterward she wrote this hymn.

About these words, her brother said:

> In the course of a long ministry, I hope I have been permitted to see some of the fruit of my labor, but I feel that far more has been done by a single hymn of my sister's.

Yes, Billy Graham's message of the twentieth and early twenty-first centuries echoes Dr. Malan's message to Charlotte Elliott in the late nineteenth century: "Come as you are!" It is a message that has spanned the past twenty-one centuries: come as you are and expect greater things!

When we come as we are to God, it is amazing. We move from status quo to get up and go!

Dr. Norman Vincent Peale wrote a famous book that outlined his philosophy, *The Power of Positive Thinking*. His appeal reached beyond his pulpit at Marble Collegiate Church in New York City to the homes and boardrooms of America.

His ten principles for dynamic living led people to truly transform their lives. His magazine, *Guidepost*, still reaches millions of people with stories of faith and inspiration. This illustrates how God's work and presence are interwoven throughout the simplicity of our daily lives. I was fortunate to attend a board of directors meeting for *Guidepost* in Southern California in January 2007. It was held in a lovely home in Anaheim. There were several world-class leaders in business, education, faith, the arts, and entertainment at the meeting. Each of them possessed a passion for living life to the fullest. They were real people living in the real world with a real faith. With their guidance, Dr. Peale's message continues to live through *Guidepost*.

Expect Greater Things Pioneers 15

Dr. Robert H. Schuller, inspired by Dr. Peale, Bishop Sheen, Dr. Graham, and modern psychology and architecture, wrote about the significance of possibility thinking. His books and the *Hour of Power* television show have reached and impacted millions of people each week for over thirty years. Now his broadcasts reach twenty-two million people each week all over the world. These people include Muslims, Hindus, Communists, as well as Christians and those who have no faith identity. Dr. Schuller's mission is to introduce the love of God to every person that he possibly can on this planet. He wants them to know the power of faith (possibility thinking) for living life to the fullest. His books and television program can help you experience the power of possibility thinking which is, in essence, living a faith lifestyle.

Dr. Schuller has been a significant mentor to me since the early 1990s. In 1998 I told him of my vision for Greater Things. In my book *Conversations on Faith*, Dr. Schuller wrote the following:

> Dr. John Myers brings to us the next generation of Possibility Thinking. It is called Greater Things! I have known John for over a decade and I can tell you that he is one of the dynamic leaders for the 21st Century. John's Greater Things principles for living will inspire you to Expect Greater Things, Grow in Greater Things and Do Greater Things with your life, family, finances, faith, business and faith community. His keynotes, writing and seminars will challenge, inspire and motivate you to make a difference."
>
> Robert H. Schuller
>
> Founding Pastor, The Crystal Cathedral

I was so happy to find that my mentor believes in the vision of Greater Things and that he endorsed it in such a great way! Why did this happen? I expected greater things!

Each of these pioneers offers to the nation and the world what I term an Expect Greater Things perspective on life. It is a perspective that states, "You can expect greater things in your life because you are connected to God! Because of that connectedness your life will be qualitatively different."

These are some of the pastoral leaders of the late twentieth century who made an Expect Greater Things mark. But there are other influencers who contributed to a broader definition of expecting greater things beyond the faith-based community.

A favorite author of millions, who is known for his Expect Greater Things message of hope, was Napoleon Hill. His landmark book *Think and Grow Rich* is a wonderfully powerful text on the subject of personal financial growth and happiness. The book reveals the secrets of success that have guided leaders such as Andrew Carnegie, Henry Ford, William Wrigley Jr., George Eastman, William Jennings Bryan, John D. Rockefeller, Thomas Edison, Woodrow Wilson, William Howard Taft, and a host of others. (*Author's note:* Women are not mentioned in this list due to the fact that the author, in his time and place, did not interview them. If his book were written today, there would be several outstanding women listed as well, such as Oprah Winfrey, Hillary Clinton, Queen Latifa, Martha Stewart, Maya Angelou, and Princess Diana.) Many of these principles are extracted from the biblical principles of excellence in living found in both the Old and New Testaments and in business principles dating back to Adam Smith's *Wealth of Nations*.

I discovered Napoleon Hill's writings and philosophy in the spring of 1993. Dr. Arthur DeKruyter, then the pastor of Oakbrook Community Church of Oakbrook, Illinois, stated to me over lunch, "Well, obviously, you have read Napoleon Hill's book *Think and Grow Rich*," to which I replied, "Actually, no I haven't." He said, "Really? Are you sure? You display each of the positive characteristics that he outlines for successful living." You can bet that I picked up a copy of the book the next day! I was certainly curious about Dr. DeKruyter's insights into my personality.

Wow! It is a fantastic book! I read it while on a cruise vacation with my family to the Bahamas. In fact, I couldn't put it down. The wisdom in that little book has been a guide for me ever since. In fact, I wrote down several of the key points and loaded them into my Day-Timer in the mid-1990s and later into my Personal Digital

Organizer. Now it is in my smart phone! The technology changes, but the principles remain time-tested and true.

Here are several of Hill's maxims I still review at least once a week. I think you will find them helpful.

The Twelve Secrets of Leadership:
1. Unwavering Courage
2. Self-Control
3. A Keen Sense of Justice
4. Definiteness of Decision
5. Definiteness of Plans
6. The Habit of Doing More Than Paid For
7. A Pleasing Personality
8. Sympathy and Understanding
9. Mastery of Detail
10. Willingness to Assume Full Responsibility
11. Cooperation
12. QQSS: Quality, Quantity, Service with Spirit

Other maxims from Hill's writings I have found useful across the years are:

- A quitter never wins and a winner never quits.
- The days of the "go-getter" have passed. He has been supplanted by the "go-giver."
- Tell the world what you intend to do, but first show it.
- Listen, don't talk, accumulate knowledge, and don't divulge information/thoughts.
- Acquire facts or secure information quietly, without disclosing your purpose.
- People who envy you will attempt to defeat you.
- Genuine wisdom is usually conspicuous through modesty and silence.
- Keep a closed mouth and open ears.
- Every powerful man has himself within his own power.
- Success requires no explanations, failure permits no alibis.

Thoughts are Things!

- Why leaders fail: unwillingness to render humble service, intemperance, emphasis of "authority" of leadership and emphasis of title.
- The seven major positive emotions: desire, faith, love, sex, enthusiasm, romance, and hope.
- Most people wish for riches, but few provide the definite plan and the burning desire which pave the road to wealth.

Hill also describes a *sixth sense* that guides people to excellence in living, relationships, and business. It is the apex of his philosophy. It can be assimilated, understood, and applied only by first mastering the other twelve principles. The sixth sense is the creative imagination through which ideas, plans, and thoughts flash into the mind. These flashes are sometimes called hunches or inspiration. Through the aid of the sixth sense, you will be warned of impending dangers in time to avoid them, and be notified of opportunities in time to embrace them. The sixth sense is a "guardian angel" who will open to you at all times the door to the temple of wisdom.

Napoleon Hill's work encourages people to expect greater things in their lives by thinking and growing rich relationally, financially, and spiritually.

When we expect greater things in our lives, it is amazing what God can do with, in, and for us! And yet I believe it is essential for people to move beyond practical faith (Sheen), the power of positive thinking (Peale), accepting Christ and finding a church home (Graham), possibility thinking (Schuller), thinking and growing rich (Hill), and expecting greater things (yours truly), to living the Greater Things lifestyle.

This lifestyle is a thought-style that is also a faith-style in God and yourself. Contemporary authors such as Dr. Wayne W. Dyer (*The Power of Intention*), Robert T. Kiyosaki (*Rich Dad, Poor Dad*), Dr. Thomas J Stanley (*The Millionaire Mind*), Paul Zane Pilzer (*Unlimited Wealth*), T. Harv Eker (*Secrets of the Millionaire Mind*), and a host of others write about the fact that thoughts are things!

Don't misunderstand what I am saying here. Expecting Greater Things is not about getting rich quick. Financial wealth might happen as a result of your outlook and the amazing network that you will develop, but it will be a by-product of living a life that expects greater things, grows in greater things, and does greater things. And even if you don't end up listed as one of *Fortune*'s Wealthiest People in the World, it won't matter. You will have an intrinsic wealth of soul, spirit, friendships, relationships, and networking that will make you the richest person in town.

This reminds me of one of my favorite movies, *It's a Wonderful Life*. The central character, George Bailey, didn't realize the wonderful life he had, based on his drafty house, low bank account, and a host of setbacks throughout his life. He felt he had let life pass him by because he had stayed to oversee the family business, a savings and loan company. But through a series of incredible circumstances and a whimsical angel named Clarence, George discovered that his life had made an astounding impact on the entire town and its citizens. In fact, he was pronounced the "richest man in town." Once his perception of his life changed, George had a Greater Things outlook on life, and he truly was the richest man in the mythical town of Bedford Falls.

If I were to ask you who won the Super Bowl for the last ten years, could you do it? If I were to ask you to name the ten best inspirational speeches you have ever heard and who they were delivered by, could you do it? Probably not. While these things are important, they are not the stuff of which true life is made.

But if I asked you to list the ten people who have influenced your life the most, my guess is that you could do it without even thinking. Relationships are what matter the most. George Bailey in *It's a Wonderful Life* was the richest man in town because of his relationship equity. How is your relationship equity? We will explore this question more fully in Chapter 9. I encourage you to visit the ExpectGreaterThings.com Web site to learn more about the people who have been pioneers of expecting greater things. Study their materials and train your mind for an Expect Greater Things lifestyle.

Next, we are going to look at the Expect Greater Things challenge. Here it is:

Do you believe that you can expect, grow in, and do greater things with your life? If so, how do you turn that belief into energy? How do you convert the energy into thought? How do you convert the thought into faith? How do you convert the faith into substance? How do you transform the substance into influence? How do you turn the influence into greater results for living?

POINTS TO PONDER

- You can expect greater things and find a great vision and dream for something larger than your life. But it might not happen overnight; in fact, it might take a long time.
- There are Greater Things pioneers who helped make faith in God and the self accessible and understandable. They downplayed the negative and accentuated the positive.

QUESTIONS FOR REFLECTION

- Who are my Greater Things pioneers?
- In what ways am I growing in my faith in God and the self in order that I can accentuate the positive?
- Which Greater Things pioneer mentioned in this chapter do I want to learn from through study and reflection?
- What will I do to experience the power of great relationships with God and others?

CHAPTER 3

THE EXPECT GREATER THINGS CHALLENGE

Do you believe that you can expect, grow, and do greater things with your life? If so:

Turn that belief into energy!
Convert the energy into thought!
Transform your thought into faith!
Convert your faith into substance!
Transform the substance into influence!
Turn the influence into greater results for living!

This chapter will explore the greater things challenge of moving from belief in God and yourself to the joyful living of a greater things lifestyle. It is born from a greater things faith-style!

EXPECTING GREATER THINGS IN YOUR LIFE THROUGH FAITH IN GOD

Did you know that God expects greater things from us? We have been put on this earth for a purpose beyond ourselves. In fact, when we reach the full potential that God has in mind for us, the results can literally change our world!

> I tell you the truth, anyone who has faith in me will do what I have been doing. He will do even greater things than these, because I am going to the Father. And I will do whatever you

21

> ask in my name, so that the Son may bring glory to the Father. You may ask me for anything in my name, and I will do it.
>
> Jesus, John 14:12–14

Wow! What a promise! Did you know that God expects you to do greater things?

Take a look at the Expect Greater Things context:

- First, Jesus is saying farewell to his disciples. They have followed him for three years. But now, the end of his ministry and his earthly life are coming to a close. So Jesus is briefing them (John 14–17) about his expectations, promises, hopes, goals, and the objectives that he has in mind. He wants them to live with the expectation that by following God that they will be able to do greater things than he, himself, had done! Wow! That sounds like a tall order, but it is possible.
- Second, Jesus is speaking to followers, not simply believers. What is the difference? A believer is someone who casually affiliates with God with little or no change in behavior. A *follower*, however, is a person committed to a different lifestyle because of their relationship with the one they are following. In this text, Jesus is stating that if a person follows him there will be a qualitative difference in the person's life! It is, in fact, a greater things difference.

Don't confuse "different lifestyle" with the do's and don'ts of religion. This is not about religiosity. In fact, it is just the opposite. It is about being freed from a legalistic, hemmed-in religion in order to reach your full, God-given potential.

God wants us to be free so that we can achieve greater things through our faith and love! He doesn't want us to be religious! He wants us to be faithful and fulfilled. What is the difference?

Years ago, the television show Saturday Night Live had a character created and played by Dana Carvey. This character was "the church lady." The church lady was dressed extremely conservatively. Her hair was gray and pulled back into a tight bun, with the forehead outlined by a widow's peak. Her take on everything under the sun was a cynical and critical, "Well, isn't that special?" The audience never once heard a positive word from her mouth. Her body language was confrontational, not loving. Her basic attitude was judgmental, not forgiving. Her whole demeanor characterized religion as being not fun and not kind. And, in fact, she was often caught in the crossfire of her religiosity and her own actions to which she was blind, but which everyone else could see. Wow! America would howl at the church lady! Why? Because anyone who has been around religious people knows at least one such church lady or man!

Such people repel others from the faith because of their religion. They do not attract people to God. I ministered as a pastor in churches for over thirty years. And, there were some amazing people in those churches! They were wonderful people of faith who truly knew what it was to lead an Expect Greater Things faith-style that led to an amazing lifestyle.

However, I came across many *churchy* people. They had the form of religion, but not the power of faith in their lives. They went through the motions, but didn't have the joy of the living God in their hearts. They were quick to point out other's faults, but didn't know how to help them past their faults to experience the love and grace of God in their lives. You see, the church lady character was not born in a vacuum.

The most shining example of the church lady was in one of my churches in Indiana where I served as the associate pastor. It happened in the early 1980s. Some visitors had come to church for the first time. It was a rainy fall day in Indiana. The church was almost full. There were few seats available. The newcomers found two seats in which to sit for the service. But just as they got comfortable and settled for worship, a lady with an umbrella came to them and said, "You are sitting in my seat." The visitors replied, "We're new here and just got settled." The church lady replied, "I said you are sitting in my seat!" The visitors replied, "We didn't see any reserved seating." To which the church lady replied, while raising her umbrella ready to strike, "I said you are sitting in my seat. Please get up and find somewhere else to sit." An usher overheard the exchange and promptly found a place for the disgruntled church lady to sit.

    Wow! I bet that visiting couple thought twice about going back to the church, no matter how good the sermon or the music was that day. Yes, the church lady's character was not born in a vacuum. The character of the church lady was born out of the do's and don'ts of religiosity. And, America laughed because each of us knows someone who acts that way. And sometimes, without knowing it, perhaps we ourselves have even acted that way! But what is the fallout?

    The good news is that, according to most polls, America's search for faith has held steady over the past seventy-five years. We do believe that organized religion has lost some of its influence since the 1950s, but the importance of faith in our personal lives has been consistent and, perhaps, even grown.

    Since 1997 church attendance in America has dropped 6 percent. In 1997, 44 percent of all Americans worshipped in a church or synagogue on a regular basis. Now, only 38 percent can be found in worship. Yet 95 percent of Americans say that they believe in God! 75 to 85 percent say that they are Christians either in the Protestant, Catholic, or Orthodox faiths. But fewer and fewer of us are attending church on a regular basis. In fact, many of us are finding new ways to explore and grow our spirituality ("Multicasting, podcasting and younger audience shake things up," by Reed Business Information, a division of Reed Elsevier, Inc., September 24, 2007).

    I predicted these trends in 1994 when I wrote my doctoral dissertation entitled, Networking in the Global Village. One section of the book declared that we were a postdenominational nation, which was on the verge of being postChristian as well. Christians can no longer afford the luxury of drawing lines in the sand, whether they be theological, denominational, philosophical, racial, political, or economic in order for a winner to stand tall or a loser to forfeit all. The Christian church cannot afford to divide into camps. It is time Christianity woke up and realized we have an entire world looking at us to see if we are authentic.

The seeker of spirituality and God does not care about doctrine, theological heritage, or denominational nomenclature. The seeker does not care whether the church is United Methodist, Roman Catholic, Pentecostal, United Church of Christ, Holiness, Presbyterian, Episcopalian, Greek Orthodox, Russian Orthodox, Baptist, or Lutheran. The seeker does want to know one thing and one thing only: Are we authentic? Are we real? Are we in love with God and in love with one another? Do we care about others more than we care about ourselves?

The seeker in the world says, "If you are authentic, fantastic! Let's go. If not, why not? I'll find a different spot to cast my lot."

My heart tells me to work in every way possible to help seekers of a greater things experience with God, and others, who are hurting, desperate, and despondent to see an authentic faith in the midst of a complicated, sophisticated, and sometimes adulterated, post-9/11 world.

People are crying out for a real spirituality in real times for real people. My experience tells me that people don't really care about the brands of the different denominations. This has been increasingly true since the late 1980s.

The following story illustrates my point.

A young family was getting ready to join a church in the fall of 2007. The family was comprised of a beautiful wife, a handsome husband, and three boys under the age of four. Wow! Talk about combustible energy! The mother said, "I was brought up Catholic and so was my husband. We moved to the area three years ago, attended a local Catholic church, but didn't like it. So we haven't been going anywhere. Recently, we started coming to this church. We want to join this church because we like the pastor and the people, and there are lots of young families starting to come here. But if I join as a United Methodist, do I have to be a United Methodist for life? What if we move and don't find a United Methodist Church we like, but find a church of a different denomination? Then what? We want an authentic experience for our family."

This young mother voiced a truth in our country: We are postdenominational. People care about whether or not they can find a practical authenticity in their spirituality. They don't care about the brand name.

By and large people don't find the label of a denomination important anymore. This has been documented since the early 1990s. We do live in a postdenominational era. This is not to say that denominations are unnecessary, or they have fully served their purpose. A statement of this nature would be premature and arrogant. Denominations are still necessary and important for the general maintenance of the variety of ministries to which God has called them. In addition, denominations speak the message of God's love in Jesus Christ to millions and millions of people, and equip these people for the purpose of missioned outreach in local, regional, national, and international arenas.

The significance of denominations is on the decline, while the importance of spirituality is on the increase in the mind of the general population. This fact was reinforced on ABC's *Good Morning America*. Charles Gibson reported that the Jewish, Roman Catholic, and Muslim religions are on the rise, but that the mainline denominations are on a sharp decline. He further reported, however, that America's search for spirituality is stronger than it has been in decades, as baby boomers and their children search for meaning after determining that material goods and career advancements don't make a complete and peace-filled life. The amazing thing about this report is that it was aired May 2, 1994. It sounds as if it could have been reported in 2007.

As we have entered the twenty-first century, people are not asking what we want *next* . . . we are asking what we want *most*! And what we want most is meaning! John Milton wrote, "There is nothing that makes men rich and strong but that which they carry inside of them. Wealth is of the heart, not of the hand." What matters is the authenticity of the experience with God and the application of it in the home, workplace, and society. If an individual church can fill that need, then people will be attracted to it. If not, then the church will simply exist to care for its own flock until the flock either moves or dies out.

People today will search for spirituality and meaning in all sorts of places. They will look for it in life-coaching, books, seminars, Web sites, movies, vacations with a purpose, and on and on! In fact, Americans are combining the faith and teachings not only of the Bible, but of the ancients.

I wrote a business plan for my company, Greater Things Enterprises, in 1999. The goal was to bring spiritual formation and spirituality to people through books, seminars, workshops, the Internet, and mass media. I was seeing ahead of the curve, and God was preparing me for the work that I am doing now. The goal was to communicate the contemporary relevance of what the ancients taught about tangible and intangible spiritual formation found in relationships, investments, philanthropy, and the soul. This is being accomplished through the writing of this series of *Expect Greater Things* books, the www.expectgreaterthings.com Web site, and the Greater Things Champions Radio Show.

But guess what? This is not a new phenomenon. This has been a long-standing issue dating back to ancient times.

Jesus said to the Jews who believed in him, "If you continue in my word, you will be my disciples. Then you will know the truth and the truth shall set you free! . . . If the Son shall set you free, you will be free indeed" (John 8:31, 32, 36).

It is interesting to note that Jesus was dealing with the organized religion of his time: the Jewish faith. He constantly was talking with the religious leaders about having an authentic faith, not a plastic religiosity. He even called some of the religious leaders of his time, who cared more about appearance than substance, whitewashed tombs. Ouch! Kind of like Dana Carvey's church lady!

Jesus had several people who followed him to hear his teachings and see his miracles. Many of them believed that he was an amazing teacher, and some even believed that he might be the Messiah. But Jesus wanted them to do more than believe; he wanted them to achieve greater things with their lives so that they would be fulfilled and God would be glorified. Jesus wanted the best for them!

Following God *begins* with belief, but believing is not enough. Believing is only the beginning of an entire greater things faith-style that can powerfully change our lifestyle. Jesus outlines the key to this transformation. It is a progressive regenerating process that involves:

- Continuing in God's Word
- Being disciples and followers
- Knowing the truth
- Being free to live a greater things lifestyle

The Greater Things Challenge for the disciples was this: did they expect, grow in and do greater things?

Absolutely! According to the Bible, after Jesus was crucified, died, was buried, arose from the dead, appeared to over five hundred people, and ascended into heaven to sit with God the Father, he followed through with the promise of sending the Holy Spirit to those who followed him. You can read about this in Acts 2. It is great stuff! But this is what happened in Acts and in much of the rest of the New Testament with the followers of Jesus. They did greater things!

Think about it!

On the day of Pentecost over 3000 people decided to follow God! As a result . . .

- The church was born. The world would never be the same.
- The Gospels of Matthew, Mark, Luke, and John, as well as the book of Acts and the remaining books of the New Testament, were written in order to tell the story of Jesus Christ and the early church.
- Since the New Testament era, the message of God's love has shaped history and changed lives.
- How did it all happen? The disciples and early followers of Jesus Christ lived with a greater things frame of mind! They continued in God's word, they became disciples, they knew

the truth, and the truth set them free to expect, grow, and do greater things to the glory of God!

THE EXPECT GREATER THINGS CHALLENGE TODAY

How can we as individuals experience an Expect Greater Things frame of mind? How can we power-train our mind for thinking outside the box? How can we move past the status quo of mortgage payments, credit card debt, mundane day-to-day living, to the power of rising above the dredge of life to see the phenomenal power for living that each of us has at our fingertips?

Jesus coaches us with the answers to these questions:

First, believing is not enough if you want to expect, grow, and do greater things with your life!

Second, it is essential to study the Bible, ancient writings of wisdom, and life strategy, as well as excellent teachings from the classics and contemporary writers and thinkers. This will help inform you, and enable you to form a wonderful power-filled faith that meets life.

Third, as you study and grow, as well as talk with others on the journey, you will know the truth for your life. You will live with an empowered confidence. You will think of living life in ways you never thought possible before. You will find yourself on adventures that you would never have dreamt possible. People you would never have known will appear before you just when you need them, and your dreams and goals will be realized because you are literally expecting greater things!

Fourth, you will know the truth of why you are here, and you will be free to achieve your God-given purpose! So,

> Turn that belief into energy!
> Convert the energy into thought!
> Transform your thought into faith!
> Convert your faith into substance!
> Transform the substance into influence!
> Turn the influence into greater results for living!

POINTS TO PONDER

- Turn belief into energy!
- Convert the energy into thought!
- Transform the thought into faith!
- Convert the faith into substance!
- Transform the substance into influence!
- Turn the influence into greater results for living!
- God expects greater things from us.
- We have been put on this earth for a purpose beyond ourselves.
- When we reach the full potential that God has in mind for us, the results can literally change our world!

QUESTIONS FOR REFLECTION

- How can I experience an Expect Greater Things frame-of-mind?
- How can I power-train my mind for thinking outside the box?
- How can I move past the status quo to the power of seeing the phenomenal power for living that is at my fingertips?

CHAPTER 4

EXPECT GREATER THINGS CHAMPIONS

How do I know that this process of expecting greater things works? It has worked in my life countless times in ways that would be otherwise impossible.

Let me share three of these personal experiences with you!

A LADY NAMED IDA

I was fortunate to matriculate to Purdue University and receive a scholarship for singing in the Purdue Varsity Glee Club. Purdue doesn't have a music school, but they have one of the finest men's glee clubs in the United States. I was offered a scholarship in my senior year of high school and chose to go to Purdue to study mass communications and interpersonal communications. This was over and against an offer from the School of Music from Indiana University for a full scholarship in voice. But I asked God for guidance and decided to attend Purdue.

The Varsity Glee Club often finished each academic year with a trip overseas. In 1977 the trip was to Europe! This was my first trip across the pond called the Atlantic Ocean. How exciting. We landed, toured, and sang in London. Next up was a shaky trip across the English Channel where I had my first "almost" experience with seasickness. Here's a tip: if you think you are getting seasick go up on deck where you can get some fresh air and look at the horizon. Do not stay inside.

Once we crossed the English Channel and landed on the French shore, we boarded buses bound for Paris. This bus trip to Paris would be the first step of many that would change my life. It was on this trip that I met a woman named Ida.

Ida was one of many Purdue glee club supporters who supplemented the cost of the trip for glee club members by paying an inflated travel fee so that she could accompany the glee club and travel to Europe with us. Ida was eighty-six years old, well traveled, and a 1914 graduate of Purdue University! Wow! She was also the first woman high school principal in the state of Indiana. She was truly a renaissance woman.

The temperature in the bus was rather cool. I had gone to the front of the bus to talk with the director of the glee club. On my way back I noticed an older woman who looked as if she were shivering. I introduced myself and asked her if she would like a blanket. She said, "Yes. That is so kind of you. My name is Ida!" She reached out her hand, took mine, and patted my hand three times. Her handshake defied her age. The gleam in her blue eyes communicated a love for life and people. Her smile was genuine and purposeful. I opened the blanket and placed it on her, and she said thanks.

The group arrived in Paris and unloaded at the hotel. It was a lovely hotel in the heart of the city. We were instructed that dinner would be served at 7 PM sharp, and to not be late. Well, guess who was five minutes late! You guessed it. I showed up and every seat in the dining room was filled, except one. It was the one next to Ida.

We became fast friends in Paris at dinner that evening. She told me about her husband, children, and living on the campus of Ball State University. She told me how she loved traveling around the world. In fact, she carried a little plastic loose-leaf notebook with her everywhere she went on her travels, in which she made notes, and drew pictures of monuments, buildings, and such like. She wrote about people that she had met, and her impressions and opinions of the culture.

Ida asked me lots of questions about my life, family, upbringing, dreams for the future, and vision for what I wanted to accomplish in my life. I told her that I committed my life fully to God when I was sixteen and that I believed God called me to be a spiritual leader. I related stories to her about how God had answered prayers and given me a variety of personal experiences to underscore this sense of call. And I told her that I had just completed my first year of preaching in a small church in Colburn, Indiana as a student pastor, while attending Purdue University. She asked me how old I was when I started as the pastor of the tiny church. "Nineteen," was my reply. She chuckled, patted my hand, and said, "That is wonderful!"

We finished dinner and left the table as friends.

The trip through Europe in May of 1977 was wonderful. In June of 1977, when I was at home with my parents for the summer, I received a letter from Ida. It read as follows:

> Dear John,
>
> What a wonderful trip we had in Europe. The Glee Club was wonderful in each of their performances. The best part of the trip was meeting you!
>
> I have been praying and searching for someone to whom I can give the gift of travel. I have been looking for five years. Because of your passion and vision for the future I am giving you this gift. You can travel anywhere in the world you choose. I have specifically thought of the Holy Land for you. I want you to be the best minister in the block.
>
> Call me so we can discuss this and make plans for your trip.
>
> Fondly,
>
> Ida

Wow! I read the letter to my parents. Their jaws dropped. We all decided that I should call her right away.

I placed the call. She invited me to her home to meet her husband Myron. So I drove to Muncie, Indiana, and spent time there learning the details of her travel ideas.

For two years I prepared for the first trip. My studies included classes in ancient Egypt and Mesopotamia at Purdue University. I also spent a year studying ancient Israel.

In 1978 I spent six weeks traveling in Egypt, Jordan, Israel, Greece, and Turkey. It was an amazing experience from which I learned about the culture, the history, the current socio-economic, and political scene for each area I visited. And, of course, the trip was extremely inspirational. It greatly shaped my faith, and I truly began to understand what it meant to expect greater things. I wrote, directed, and produced a documentary entitled *In the Footsteps of Jesus* as a result of this travel experience.

There was a letter from Ida waiting for me when I returned from the trip. It was the beginning of my senior year at Purdue. Ida wrote, "Now that you have traveled you will be the best minister in the block. But I want you to be the best minister in the square mile. Here is a check for you to do with as you please, but I want you to use it for travel. Fondly, your friend, Ida."

I was amazed. I called her and she suggested a European study trip. So, in 1981, after spending several weeks at Purdue studying various countries, I traveled to Europe. It was an amazing adventure.

In 1982 Ida sent me to China. I studied over twenty-eight books on the history, religion, politics, culture, and the like. This was a trip sponsored by the Divinity School at Duke University (where I attended graduate school), and the trip resulted in a documentary that I wrote, directed, and produced entitled *Focus on China*.

As the years progressed, Ida and I continued our friendship. My life was filled with the joys of raising two small children and spending time with family and friends, as well as serving churches in Fort Wayne and South Bend, Indiana. We wrote letters to one another every week. I visited her often, even after she was moved from her home on the campus of Ball State University to an extended care facility.

Ida lived to be ninety-nine years old, and was one of my best friends. I performed a celebration of her life at her home church in Muncie. Over 200 people attended her funeral—a large number for a woman her age. The event served as a testament to a person who had lived with an Expect Greater Things frame of mind, lifestyle, and faith.

You might say, "Well, John, you were just at the right place at the right time." I would say, "You are right! But who put me there? Why me at that point in time? Why Ida?" It was because she and I both lived with an Expect Greater Things hope.

Amazing things happen when we live with focus and expectation. Life brings us the right people at the right time to fulfill our visions and purposes on this earth! This is faith in God in action.

A vision and goal that I have for the future through the Greater Things Institute is to create a fund for sponsoring travel for students who have a sense of calling and purpose in their lives. The calling could be in the field of education, business, faith, politics, medicine, or entertainment. Wouldn't it be wonderful to find Expect Greater Things champions who could be given the gift of travel so they can become the best teachers, business leaders, physicians, athletes, and spiritual leaders in the square block and then the square mile! This would be the Ida Travel Award offered through the Greater Things Institute.

The above story about Ida is one of over a hundred that have happened to me since I became a person of faith. I will share one more story, which will knock your socks off! Actually, there are two stories in one that underscore the power of living with focus and an Expect Greater Things faith.

EXPECT GREATER THINGS AND EARN A DOCTORAL DEGREE IN RUSSIA

In the Fall of 1991, I was invited to participate in a postdoctoral study group through the United Theological Seminary in Dayton, Ohio. The president of the seminary was Dr. Leonard Sweet, a theologian, historian, and futurist. Dr. Sweet also invited sixteen leading pastors from various denominations. At the time, I served on the seminary's board of advisors as a young leader. Upon receiving the invitation, I called Dr. Sweet and said, "Len, I am honored and would love to participate, but I don't have a doctorate, so how can I be in a postdoctorate study group?" He laughed and said, "We will make the study tour your doctoral work!"

I had been praying and thinking about how I would earn my doctorate. I didn't want to do a conventional doctoral study— I wanted to do something different that could impact not only on my life, but the lives of others also. Well, God had the perfect outline in mind, and with Len Sweet acting as the conduit, God revealed that outline to me by enabling my first trip to Russia. Dr. Robert H. Schuller, members of the Churches United in Global Missions, and the Russian officials, dignitaries, educators, politicians, business leaders, educators, and religious leaders were the conduit for the second part of the work. Russia, from 1992 to 1997, would be where I would study, travel, work, and write—earning, in the process, my doctoral degree in 1994.

From 1992 to 1997 I made eight trips to Russia. At first the trips were with twenty or more people. Later, I found myself traveling with two others on a trip of diplomacy that involved the United States Embassy, the Russian Orthodox Church, and the mayor of Moscow. And from 1995 to 1997, I traveled on my own to meet with leaders in Christianity, education, and business. The results of the experience were many, including:

- Creating the first Sunday school curriculum in the thousand-year history of the Russian Orthodox Church.
- Coaching church leaders on how to bring faith to those outside the church, after many decades of communism and atheism.
- Helping to create the Russian Farm Project that taught privatization and agribusiness principles using seed potatoes.
- Helping to create privatized sawmills, bakeries, and dairies.
- Writing a curriculum of business ethics and values for the first Masters of Business Administration program in St. Petersburg, Russia.
- Helping to establish a microlending institution for entrepreneurs.

These trips were expensive. Living on a pastor's salary and serving at a local church in South Bend, Indiana, how did I pay for these trips and the doctoral work? I expected greater things!

I contacted people I knew throughout the nation and invited them to share in the journey by helping to sponsor these activities. Periodic newsletters went out to each supporter, and when I earned my doctorate, personal letters of thanks went to each sponsor. I expected greater things and people who were already Greater Things champions were happy to help out! My thanks still goes out to them.

You see, there are Greater Things champions just waiting to help you on your journey so that you can fulfill your God-given potential when you live by faith. The journey is amazing!

So that is part one of a two-part story. Part two is this:

EXPECT GREATER THINGS AND BE THE CONDUIT FOR A MEETING WITH MIKHAIL GORBACHEV

My first trip to Russia was in April of 1992. In a planning meeting for that trip in October 1991, Len Sweet asked the group the following question: does anyone know how to get a meeting with Mikhail Gorbachev? Everyone looked at each other with blank stares. No one spoke up. We decided to make it a matter of prayer.

January 1992 placed me in Garden Grove, California, for a five-day continuing education event titled *International School of Christian Communication* at the Crystal Cathedral. It would be a week of one-on-one mentoring from Dr. Robert H. Schuller, Dr. Frank Freed, Dr. Bruce Larson, and many other great leaders and teachers. There were twenty of us in the sessions, and a great deal was learned. But the serendipity wasn't the event, but what happened on the way to the event.

My budget for continuing education and travel wasn't large; in fact, it was a bit sparse. My administrative assistant in Indiana booked me for five nights at the Hilton Suites for $99.00 per night. I could just see my balance going down to nothing in my travel and continuing education account. So I decided to shop around before checking into the hotel.

Spotting a Marriott Residence Inn, I drove my rental car into the driveway and parked. I was wearing a two piece double-breasted suit, a dress shirt, tie, and dress shoes. When I approached the front desk, I mentioned that I was shopping for a great deal for the week. The desk attendant picked up the phone, dialed, and asked a gentleman to come down to meet me.

The gentleman was the CEO of the Western Rim Management Corporation. He was in charge of that particular property, along with many others. We went on a walking tour of the property and talked about why I was in Orange County. I asked him several questions about his work and his passions in life.

He told me that he was working on establishing a five-star hotel in formerly communist Russia (Expect Greater Things!). I said, "Really?" He said, "Yes, in Moscow." I said, "I'm going to be in Moscow in April." He asked, "What for?" I told him that I was traveling with a group of spiritual leaders. He asked what we wanted to do while we were there. I said, "Well one thing that we want to do is meet with Mikhail Gorbachev, but we aren't quite sure how to get in touch with him and set it up." "Really?" he replied. "Meet me tomorrow at 7:30 for breakfast and I will introduce you to two of my associates from Russia. They might be able to help out."

Expect Greater Things! The next morning I met with John, the CEO, Alexander, and Sasha. Alexander was a leading Russian in finance. Sasha was the nephew of the former KGB head. They both knew Mikhail Gorbachev. After talking about who was in the postdoctoral study group and the mission of the group, it was determined that they would help establish a meeting with Gorbachev. I took their information and gave them Len Sweet's information.

On April 24, 1992, sixteen clergy from the United States and one from Korea met with Mikhail Gorbachev for ninety minutes in Moscow at the Gorbachev Foundation. This was less than a year after the fall of communism and after Gorbachev stepped down from power over the Soviet Union. It was less than a year after the Cold War ended.

Mikhail Gorbachev asked our group to speak to the spiritual nature of human beings. He said that since we no longer had a common enemy in each other through the Cold War, that we would now have to look inwardly to ourselves. He said that spiritual and environmental needs were the most important things we could focus on as we prepared for the twenty-first century.

We concluded the meeting by learning that Gorbachev was baptized as a child in the Russian Orthodox Church. His mother

and grandmother taught him about the faith. When asked if he believed in Christ, the former leader of the Communist world sidestepped the question with the agility of a master politician. However, when we offered to pray with him that his mission would succeed, he gladly accepted. So we stood in a circle, hand-in-hand with each other and Mr. Gorbachev, and prayed that God's guidance and grace be upon Mikhail Gorbachev's life, mission, and spirit.

Our postdoctoral group gathered together at the Radisson Hotel in Moscow shortly after our meeting with Mikhail Gorbachev. Len Sweet said, "We want to thank John Myers for making the contact with President Gorbachev. Because of his networking, we were able to have the meeting." Expect Greater Things!

What is the likelihood that out of all the hotels in southern California, I would visit the one that had exactly the three people I needed to meet in order to get a meeting with President Gorbachev? The mathematical odds are huge!

Expect Greater Things and greater things happen!

You might have seen Mikhail Gorbachev on Robert H. Schuller's *Hour of Power*. I was honored to introduce Dr. Schuller to President Gorbachev. The two have become friends, and I am sure that Dr.

Schuller's possibility thinking is making an impact on Mr. Gorbachev. We can pray so!

So the question is this: Do you Expect Greater Things? Are you living with an Expect Greater Things attitude? Are you looking to connect the cosmic dots through your faith? The Bible tells us that if we have the faith of a mustard seed, we can move mountains! I know that is true.

So we know it is true. Greater Things can be accomplished through our lives so that God can be glorified and lives can be impacted. But what might stop us from living in this reality? What are some Greater Things stoppers?

Chapter 5 will explore some Greater Things Stoppers.

POINTS TO PONDER

- Greater Things champions are waiting to help you on your journey so that you can fulfill your God-given potential as you live by faith.
- The journey is amazing!
- Expect Greater Things and greater things will happen!

QUESTIONS FOR REFLECTION

- Who is a Greater Things champion in my life?
- For whom can I be a Greater Things champion?
- Am I Expecting Greater Things? How?
- Am I living with an Expect Greater Things attitude?
- Am I looking to connect the cosmic dots through my faith?

CHAPTER 5

GREATER THINGS STOPPERS

> All human quarrels are at the bottom symptoms of a broken peace with God. No man or woman can truly live at peace until he or she has signed a peace treaty with God.
> J. C. Fischer (noted psychiatrist)

Do you remember the movie and the novel *Forrest Gump*? The movie became a classic starring Tom Hanks as Forrest Gump. In fact, in 1994 he won Best Actor at the Academy Awards for this role. Another character in the movie, Lieutenant Dan, played by Gary Sinise, beautifully and poignantly illustrates J. C. Fischer's insight: no matter how driven, no matter how decorated, no matter the family background, no matter what . . . , unless we have signed a peace treaty with God, we cannot be at peace with ourselves. If we are not at peace with ourselves, we will not be at peace with others. If we have no peace, then we cannot expect greater things in our lives.

This part of the story starts with Forrest enlisting in the army. Forrest befriends on the bus a young black man named Benjamin Buford from the small town of Bayou la Batre, Alabama. Benjamin, who goes by the nickname Bubba, tells Forrest how much he loves cooking shrimp and that before he was drafted into the army, he had planned to buy his own shrimp boat!

Forrest and Bubba are deployed to Vietnam, where they meet their commanding officer, Lieutenant Dan Taylor, whom Forrest refers to as Lieutenant Dan. While on patrol, Bubba proposes that he and Forrest go into the shrimping business after finishing their time in the army. Forrest agrees.

After several uneventful months, their platoon gets ambushed by the Viet Cong, and several soldiers are wounded and killed. In the confusion, Forrest is initially ordered to retreat, and he is separated from the rest of his platoon. But driven by his concern for Bubba, he runs back to look for him. Instead, Forrest finds Lieutenant Dan and several other wounded soldiers, and he carries them to safety before resuming his search for Bubba. Forrest finally finds a badly wounded Bubba and manages to carry him away from the combat area before it is hit by a napalm air strike. Sadly, Bubba dies of his injuries soon after.

Forrest himself is shot in the buttocks during the incident and eventually recovers in an army hospital. Lieutenant Dan is in the bed next to his, having lost his lower legs to injuries. Lieutenant Dan is angry at Forrest for supposedly cheating him out of his destiny to die honorably in battle (like several of his ancestors) and leaving him a cripple.

The dialogue that follows illustrates his frustration with life:

Lt. Dan: Now, you listen to me. We all have a destiny. Nothing just happens; it's all part of a plan. I should have died out there with my men! But now, I'm nothing but a cripple! A legless freak. Look! Look! Look at me! Do you see that? Do you know what it's like not to be able to use your legs?

Forrest: Well . . . Yes, sir, I do.

Lt. Dan: Did you hear what I said? You cheated me. I had a destiny. I was supposed to die in the field! With honor! That was my destiny! And you cheated me out of it! You understand what I'm saying, Gump? This wasn't supposed to happen. Not to me. I had a destiny. I was Lieutenant Dan Tyler.

To which Forrest replies, "You're still Lieutenant Dan!"

Time passes and Forrest is awarded the Congressional Medal of Honor. He appears on *The Dick Cavett Show*. After the show Forrest leaves the studio, and waiting outside for him is Lieutenant Dan. Look at the dialogue:

Lt. Dan: They gave you the Congressional Medal of Honor.

Forrest: Now that's Lieutenant Dan. Lieutenant Dan!
Lt. Dan: They gave you the Congressional Medal of Honor!
Forrest: Yes sir, they sure did.
Lt. Dan: They gave you, an imbecile, a moron who goes on television and makes a fool out himself in front of the whole damn country, the Congressional Medal of Honor.
Forrest: Yes, sir.
Lt. Dan: Well, then, that's just perfect! Yeah, well I just got one thing to say to that. Goddamn bless America.

Have you ever known anyone with Lieutenant Dan's disposition? Have you ever felt or acted that way yourself? These are Greater Things Stoppers: bitterness, jealousy, envy, anger. It is tough to know God's peace when there is so much negativity and criticism. It is tough and impossible to expect greater things when there is no peace.

During New Year's Eve Lieutenant Dan and Forrest have the following exchange about God:

Lt. Dan: Have you found Jesus yet, Gump?
Forrest: I didn't know I was supposed to be looking for him, sir.
Lt. Dan: That's all these cripples, down at the VA, that's all they ever talk about. Jesus this and Jesus that. Have I found Jesus? They even had a priest come and talk to me. He said God is listening, but I have to help myself. Now, if I accept Jesus into my heart, I'll get to walk beside him in the Kingdom of Heaven. Did you hear what I said? Walk beside him in the Kingdom of Heaven. Well, kiss my crippled ass. God is listening. What a crock.

I have found God working on me the most when I am the most frustrated with Him; when I ask the toughest question, God wants me to find the best answers. C. S. Lewis, the great spiritual writer, penned these words:

> We are like blocks of stone, out of which the sculptor carves the forms of men. The blows of his chisel, which hurt so much, are what makes us perfect.

So let's read on and see what happens to Lieutenant Dan. Forrest tells the lieutenant that he, Forrest, is going to be a shrimp boat captain to honor Bubba. Lieutenant Dan responds in his normal fashion . . .

Lt. Dan: Now hear this! Private Gump here is gonna be a shrimp boat captain. Well, I tell you what, Gilligan, the day that you are a shrimp boat captain, I will come and be your first mate.

Forrest: Okay.

Lt. Dan: If you're ever a shrimp boat captain, that's the day I'm an astronaut.

Sure enough, Forrest buys a shrimp boat. He is new and not very good at this, but read on . . .

Forrest: I only caught five.

Old Shrimper: A couple more, you can have yourself a cocktail. Hey, you ever think about namin' this old boat?

Forrest (voice-over): I'd never named a boat before, but there was only one I could think of . . . The most beautiful name in the whole wide world: Jenny.

So Forrest continues shrimping, and one day a big surprise occurs . . .

Forrest: Lieutenant Dan, what are you doing here?

Lt. Dan: Well, I thought I'd try out my sea legs.

Forrest: Well, you ain't got no legs, Lieutenant Dan.

They work together and have the worst time ever catching shrimp. Lieutenant Dan comes up with a wry suggestion . . .

Lt. Dan: Well, maybe you should just pray for shrimp.

Forrest (voice-over): So I went to church every Sunday . . . Sometimes Lieutenant Dan came, too. Though I think he left the praying up to me.

Forrest: No shrimp.

Lt. Dan: Where the hell's this God of yours?

Forrest (voice-over): It's funny Lieutenant Dan said that, 'cause right then, God showed up.

There is a huge storm. Lieutenant Dan climbs on top of the mast of the shrimp boat and screams and yells at God. It is a dramatic scene. I remember watching it and thinking, that is a sure way to get struck dead by lightening! I have been on my boat, Greater Things, on the Atlantic Ocean during a lightening storm. Believe me, you don't want to be caught in an electrical storm in the ocean or in the Gulf of Mexico! But Lieutenant Dan didn't care. He threw caution to the wind, the moment being a spiritual wrestling match between him and God!

Lieutenant Dan was sick of life. Things hadn't gone as planned or as he had hoped for, and he was sick of it working out badly. The vacuum within him could only be filled one way.

After the storm stops, Lieutenant Dan jumps into the water. While backstroking, the ensuing dialogue with Forrest occurs:

Lt. Dan: Forrest, I never thanked you for saving my life.

Forrest (voice-over): He never actually said so, but I think he made his peace with God

Let us revisit the quote that started this chapter:

"All human quarrels are at the bottom symptoms of a broken peace with God. No man or woman can truly live at peace until he or she has signed a peace treaty with God" (Fischer 1951).

What breaks our peace with God? Psychologists will tell us that it is cognitive dissonance—that is, knowing but not doing the right thing, and being aware of the fact. This situation creates imbalance and dissonance within us. In musical terms dissonance is the opposite of harmony and melody. It is like the sound of fingernails scratching across a chalkboard.

Let me ask you a question. Have you ever driven a few miles above the speed limit on the highway and stepped on the brakes or lifted your foot off of the accelerator upon seeing a patrol car? That action is an indication and result of cognitive dissonance. On the one hand, you know it is customarily safe to go between five to nine miles over the speed limit. Yet when you see a police officer, you instinctively know that you could get pulled over and ticketed for violating the speed limit.

This reminds me of a story I heard about Dale Rooks, a school crossing guard in Florida who tried everything to get cars to slow down at the school zone. Nothing worked until he took a blow dryer and wrapped it in electrical tape, making it look like a radar gun. Dale pointed this device at the cars, and it was incredible how quickly the drivers hit the brakes. "It's almost comical," Dale said. "It's amazing how well it works."

I recently moved to the town of Tequesta (near Jupiter) in northern Palm Beach County, Florida. It is a picturesque village surrounded by the Loxahatchee River, the Hobe Sound, the Jupiter Inlet, the Intercoastal Waterway, and the Atlantic Ocean. There is a lovely lighthouse that is the oldest structure in the county. The area is not hampered by traffic jams, and the traffic moves smoothly. In fact, after 8 p.m. it is unusual to find another car on the residential neighborhood roads.

Not long ago, shortly after I had moved into my home, I was following my "five to nine miles an hour over the speed limit" rule. I was returning from the drugstore. Suddenly I noticed a police car with flashing lights behind me. I looked around to see who was in trouble. Because there was no one else on the road, it had to be me! So I pulled over. The officer said, "Sir, you are new to town, aren't you?" I said, "Yes. How'd you know?" He said, "We know our cars and our villagers. Welcome to town. We drive the posted speed limit on our streets, Sir. It keeps everybody safe. Here is a warning. Have a safe night and welcome to Tequesta."

I was amazed. It was actually kind of comforting. Talk about small-town America! How nice. Guess what? I drive within the speed limit throughout the area, and I seem to get everywhere in about the same time. But I will be honest: When the officer told me that I was speeding, I felt a twinge of guilt. Then when he said that everyone followed the posted limit, and that that was the village norm, I felt comfort in realizing that fact.

God doesn't want us to live a guilt-ridden life. He wants us to live a life that follows the "village" norm. Guilt is an Expect Greater Things stopper. God wants us to live life freely within His norms. Listen to the word of the Psalmist: "Count yourself lucky, how happy you must be—you get a fresh start, your slate's wiped clean. Count yourself lucky—God holds nothing against you and you're holding nothing back from Him" (Psalm 32:1–2). That's how I felt when the officer handed me the warning ticket: pure relief! God wants us to live without the weight of guilt and cognitive dissonance, even though we sometimes choose to go our own way instead of following God's.

The first time that I remember having that "fingernails on the chalkboard" feeling was when I was five years old. Our family lived on a main street in downtown Marion, Indiana. There was a fair amount of traffic. It was a winter day, and I had become bored playing in the backyard in the snow. My friends had gone home, and I had nothing to do. So I decided to go the alley in back of our house and make slush snowballs with rocks in them. I took them around to the front of our house and sat on the porch watching cars go by at about thirty miles per hour. I decided to see if I could hit a car or two with my snow-slush balls. I threw one . . . missed . . . splat . . . right on the street. I threw a second one . . . missed . . . splat . . . on the sidewalk. Then, miracle of miracles, I threw a third . . . nice arch . . . good distance . . . car . . . windshield . . . splat . . . crack . . . woman's scream . . . brakes . . . car door open . . . .

I don't remember anything after that because I ran from the porch and hid in the alley in back of a friend's house. It seemed like hours passed. I was cold. I was afraid. I was ashamed and worried that I had hurt somebody.

The next thing I knew, my mother, a woman, and a police officer were looking for me. I was busted and in a heap of trouble. And that was the first cognitive-dissonance experience I remember!

The New Testament writer of the book of James says: "Sin is knowing the right thing to do and not doing it" (4:17). Wow! I knew that I should not have packed the snowballs with slush and rocks and thrown them at cars. The cost could have been a human life or a car accident. Fortunately, my action only resulted in a broken windshield and weeks of personal downtime. And it taught me a lesson: think before you act.

Whether we call it cognitive dissonance or sin, they are one and the same. The Bible teaches us that we need God's grace and forgiveness to experience peace with Him.

"There is no difference, for all have sinned and fallen short of the glory of God, and are justified freely by His grace through the redemption that came by Christ Jesus . . . for those who believe" (Romans 3:23). This is a wonderful teaching! Because God loves us so much, He forgives us for our sins: "But God demonstrates his own love for us in this: While we were yet sinners, Christ died for us"

(Romans 5:8–11). But forgiveness is not automatic. We must make our peace with God. Again we can learn from the Psalmist: "When I kept it all inside, my bones turned to powder, my words became daylong groans. The pressure never let up; all the juices of my life dried up" (Psalm 32:3–4). Have you ever felt that way? That is an Expect Greater Things stopper: holding it inside and not making peace with God.

I grew up in a family of five children. I have an older sister Carol who is sixteen years my senior. The second oldest is my brother Bill. He is eleven years older. The middle child in the family is my brother Royal (nine years older). The second youngest is my sister Mara who is six years older than me. My mother and father kept to a busy life with the family and the business. My mother always wanted a nice piano so that the children could take piano lessons. So Dad bought a beautiful piano.

One day, two years before I was born. The name Zorro appeared on the piano. It had been carved into the wood with a pocket knife! Family folklore tells me that my parents held a grand inquisition for my sister Carol, my brothers Bill and Royal, and my sister Mara, who was four at the time. No one fessed up. In fact, the story of Zorro lived as family folklore well into my forties! It was always assumed that Bill had done it. He liked to work with his pocket knife, and he took piano lessons. The forensic evidence pointed to him.

This all changed one night at a Christmas party, when all five of us grown-up siblings were at home with Mother after Dad had passed away. My sister Mara, who had recently made peace with God, said to my brother Bill, "I have a confession to make!" Bill said, "You wrote Zorro in the piano." The whole family heard a loud laugh coming from the kitchen. Then, Bill and Mara came out, and she said, "Ya'all, I have a confession to make. It wasn't Bill. It was me. I carved Zorro into the piano. You see, I wanted to play Scrabble and you wouldn't let me. You said, 'You don't know how to spell.' So I decided to show you and spell Zorro on the piano. And I have carried it ever since." The whole family laughed, hooted, and hollered. It was one of the funniest and most refreshing memories that I have of my family. My brother Bill said, "See, I told you guys!" Mara and Bill laughed and hugged. My mother was amazed. But if you asked Mara, who now lives in Georgia, how she felt after her confession, she would tell you "relieved!" She had made her peace with God, and she wanted to set the record straight.

Breaking the peace with others, with ourselves, or with God takes a toll on us. Whether it is something as silly as a childhood prank that adds to family folklore or something more serious like cheating on a test, fixing the books in a corporation, cheating on a spouse or loved one, saying hurtful things against another person, or whatever the case may be, breaking the peace takes a toll. That's why the Psalmist wrote, "When I kept it all inside, my bones turned to powder, my words became daylong groans. The pressure never let up; all the juices of my life dried up" (Psalm 32:3–4).

Jesus said that if we forgive the sins of others against us, that God in heaven will forgive our sins. But if we choose not to do so, then God will not forgive us our sins (Matthew 6:15).

So what do we do with the guilt and sin that so easily entangle us? How do we lose the weight of guilt so that we can freely expect greater things? The Psalmist writes, "Then I let it all out; I said, 'I'll make a clean breast of my failures to God'" (Psalm 32:5). Suddenly the pressure was gone! My guilt dissolved, my sin disappeared. And St. John says, "If we confess our sins, he who is faithful and just will forgive us our sins and cleanse us from all unrighteousness" (John 1:9–10).

This is an Expect Greater Things way of living life at peace with God. It is significantly different from living in a world full of greater things stoppers that are measured by law and brokenness instead of grace and healing.

A BRIEF HISTORY ON THE ORIGIN OF THE WRITTEN LAW, OLD TESTAMENT LAW, AND THE NEW COMMANDMENTS FOR GREATER THINGS LIVING

Since the beginning of time and the written civilization, human beings have needed boundaries for a peaceful society. The earliest of these writings was the Code of Hammurabi that dates back to 1792 B.C. The code is carved in stone, which was discovered in 1901; it is housed at the Louvre Museum in Paris, France. I have seen this stone, and it is an amazing artifact.

Hammurabi was the King of Babylon from about 1792 B.C. to 1750 B.C. His code is inscribed on a huge stone eight meters tall in the Akkadian language. This first written code of law had 282 statutes (Gavel2Gavel.com/codeofhammurabi).

This process of creating boundaries for societal behavior continued through the ages. There are 613 laws in the Old Testament. The best known are the Ten Commandments found in Exodus, Chapter 20, and Deuteronomy, Chapter 5. But these are not just for societal behavior. They are designed to create positive boundaries so that the person of faith can not only have a dynamic relationship with God, but he or she can have personal peace and peace with the neighbors as well. Once this is established, then greater things can happen. If you haven't read the Ten Commandments in a while, here is a refresher . . .

20:1 And God spoke all these words:

20:2 I am the Lord your God, who brought you out of Egypt, out of the land of slavery.

20:3 You shall have no other gods before me.

20:4 You shall not make for yourself an idol in the form of anything in heaven above or on the earth beneath or in the waters below.

20:5 You shall not bow down to them or worship them; for I, the Lord your God, am a jealous God, punishing the children for the sin of the fathers to the third and fourth generation of those who hate me,

20:6 but showing love to a thousand generations of those who love me and keep my commandments.

20:7 You shall not misuse the name of the Lord your God, for the Lord will not hold anyone guiltless who misuses his name.

20:8 Remember the Sabbath day by keeping it holy.

20:9 Six days you shall labor and do all your work,

20:10 but the seventh day is a Sabbath to the Lord your God. On it you shall not do any work, neither you, nor your son or daughter, nor your manservant or maidservant, nor your animals, nor the alien within your gates.

20:11 For in six days the Lord made the heavens and the earth, the sea, and all that is in them, but he rested on the seventh day. Therefore the Lord blessed the Sabbath day and made it holy.

20:12 Honor your father and your mother, so that you may live long in the land the Lord your God is giving you.

20:13 You shall not murder.

20:14 You shall not commit adultery.

20:15 You shall not steal.

20:16 You shall not give false testimony against your neighbor.

20:17 You shall not covet your neighbor's house. You shall not covet your neighbor's wife, or his manservant or maidservant, his ox or donkey, or anything that belongs to your neighbor."

The fact of the matter is that it is impossible to follow all the commandments all the time. Yet the commandments underscore the significance of following God's moral and spiritual code as best we can. While it might be easy for most people not to murder, commit adultery, steal, lie against the neighbor, and the like, it might be tougher to keep the Sabbath holy. Or for some it might be difficult to honor one's mother or father. For others it might be tough not be covetous or envious. And yet others might have lied, murdered, or committed adultery.

God knew that and thus He sent his Son not to condemn the world but to save it through grace. In essence, God created us so we could do greater things with our lives! God wants us to be happy, fulfilled, and effective. So He simplified the 613 laws down to the Ten Commandments and made it easier for us to succeed by God's love and grace.

In the New Testament someone approached Jesus and asked the following question, "Of all the laws which two are the most important?" Jesus, knowing that there were 613 laws and Ten Commandments in what we now know as the Old Testament said

"Love the Lord your God with all your heart, all your mind, all your strength." Then Jesus said, "The second is to love your neighbor as you love yourself" (Matthew 22:36–39).

Wow! God simplified the number of laws from 613 to 10 to 2!

The most striking word in these two most important commandments is "love." God wants us to be love struck. Love struck by God! Love struck by God's children. What a wonderful way to describe and define ourselves as followers of God: love struck!

The spiritual life is not always smooth-cruising. In fact, no life is smooth all the time. It reminds me of my boat, *Greater Things*.

I moved my family to Florida in 2000. Our home in Fort Lauderdale was on a deep-water lot, about forty minutes by boat to the Atlantic Ocean. I decided to purchase a boat in 2002. It is a twenty-nine foot Ocean Yacht Sports Fisherman. It has two Marine-powered 350 inboard engines, a cabin, a fly bridge, a cockpit for fishing, and a bow on which to sunbath and sightsee. There is a swim platform at the back of the boat. *Greater Things* can have ten lines out in the water for fishing in the Atlantic. It is a great boat and lots of fun.

I moved to Tequesta in July 2007. I dock *Greater Things* at a friend's home on the Intercoastal Waterway. The current is strong there and the barnacle growth is much stronger than at my dock in Fort Lauderdale, off of the New River. If I don't regularly check the boat for maintenance, little and big problems can creep up; they can be very costly and time consuming to fix. Most recently, I neglected to check for barnacles at the bottom of the boat, as well as on the props and the drive shafts. This oversight resulted in sluggish performance and clogged salt water intakes.

If I had not noticed the rising water temperatures on the fly bridge instruments, I could have damaged the engines. Fortunately, I have learned to watch for these things. Experience has been my teacher! I have two new engines to prove it.

I noticed that the temperature gauges were acting up a bit. So I called a company that dives under boats, clears the barnacles, and prepares the boats for smoother cruising. They also clear the salt water intakes so the engines can be properly water cooled.

The following day I took the boat out on the water. It was no longer sluggish. It ran smoothly and efficiently. In fact, it cruised at higher speeds since the new engines were put in six months ago! It was all a matter of getting to the bottom of the problem: cleaning the barnacles from the boat.

There is a spiritual parallel here. When we become bitter, envious, jealous, greedy, lustful, proud, or angry beyond common sense, we let the barnacles encrust our soul. These barnacles become Greater Things stoppers. They can permanently damage our lives, our relationships, and our souls.

But God wants to completely clean the barnacles from our lives. God wants us to live by faith and to expect greater things! How can we do this? The key is to pray honestly and openly to God so that your barnacles can be removed. Listen to the Psalmist:

These things add up. Every one of us needs to pray; when all hell breaks loose and the dam bursts, we'll be on high ground, untouched.

God's my island hideaway, keeps danger far from the shore, throws garlands of hosannas around my neck.

Let me give you some good advice; I'm looking you in the eye and giving it to you straight . . .

PSALM 32:9–11

Don't be ornery like a horse or mule that needs bit and
bridle to stay on track.

God-defiers are always in trouble; God-affirmers find themselves
loved every time they turn around.

Celebrate God. Sing together—everyone! All you honest hearts,
raise the roof!

Have you cleared the way in your life and soul for Greater Things with God? Are you ready to make your peace treaty? It's time to clear the barnacles and get ready for Greater Things cruising and Expect Greater Things living!

> ## POINTS TO PONDER
>
> - Unless we have signed a peace treaty with God, we cannot be at peace with ourselves.
> - If we are not at peace with ourselves, we will not be at peace with others.
> - If we have no peace, then we cannot expect greater things in our lives.
> - Whether we call it cognitive dissonance or sin, they are one and the same. The Bible teaches us that we need God's grace and forgiveness to experience peace with Him.
> - Breaking the peace with others, with ourselves, or with God takes a toll on us.
> - 613 to 10 to 2
> - God wants to completely clean the barnacles from our lives.
>
> ## QUESTIONS FOR REFLECTION
>
> - Have I cleared the way in my life and soul for Greater Things with God?
> - Have I made my peace treaty with God? If not, why not?
> - Am I ready to ask God to clear the barnacles from my life? If so, then this is my prayer:

Dear God, thank you for loving me so much that you have made it possible for me to have a dynamic life by walking in faith with you. I want to live a life filled with expecting greater things through my faith in you and my relationships with others. Clear the barnacles of my life away. Give me a new power for living life to the fullest. Amen.

CHAPTER 6

EXPECT GREATER THINGS LAUNCHERS

Being at peace with God is an amazing experience that propels us to accomplish our God-given potential through faith. In this chapter I want to explore specific traits of those who expect greater things.

The first trait of an Expect Greater Things champion is that he or she lives with gratitude and courage. The second trait is the champion wishes to do more than expect something greater; a champion wants to grow in greater things!

Gratitude does four things in our lives:
1. It defeats worry and anxiety.
2. It employs prayer and thanksgiving to God for everything.
3. It enjoys God's enduring peace that passes all understanding.
4. It looks at life through the lenses of faith, not fear.

An Expect Greater Things champion has an attitude of gratitude that defeats worry and anxiety.

Worry and anxiety are realities that we, as people of faith, must acknowledge and learn to deal with constructively.

Thomas Merton (1915–1968), the great Catholic mystic, wrote, "Anxiety is a mark of spiritual insecurity."

Paramahansa Yogananda (1893–1952) is recognized as one of the greatest emissaries to the West of India's ancient wisdom. His life and teachings continue to inspire people of all races, cultures, and creeds. He wrote, "So long as we believe in our heart of hearts that our capacity is limited and we grow anxious and unhappy, we are lacking in faith. One who truly trusts in God has no right to be anxious about anything."

George Muller (1805–1898) was a Prussian-born English evangelist and philanthropist. A man of faith and prayer, he established orphanages in Bristol and founded the Scriptural Knowledge Institution for Home and Abroad. In *Signs of the Times*, he made the following observation: "The beginning of anxiety is the end of faith, and the beginning of true faith is the end of anxiety."

The opposite of anxiety is joy, energy, and peace. This comes from approaching our stress and anxiety with joy and a positive attitude. Remember that your thoughts, not your world, create your stress. So the key is to change the way you think. And an Expect Greater Things attitude of gratitude can make that happen. But how do we create this attitude?

During Emperor's Nero's rule in 64 A.D., St. Paul of Tarsus was in a Roman prison waiting to be beheaded. He wrote a joyful letter to his friends in the church in Philippi, Greece. He wrote:

> Rejoice in the Lord always. I will say it again: Rejoice! Let your gentleness be evident to all. The Lord is near. Do not be anxious about anything, but in everything, by prayer and petition, with thanksgiving, present your requests to God. Philippians 4:4–6

Wow! There he sits in prison awaiting execution, and he tells people to rejoice, to pray, to be thankful, to be gentle, to have faith that God is near, and to tell God about their needs! That is living with an attitude of gratitude.

John Guest, in *Only a Prayer Away*, writes, "When Scripture encourages us to pray without ceasing, and to cast all our care upon God, it is literally saying redirect those restless, energetic minds into a positive stream of communication with God. Turn it all into prayer."

Instead of nursing our wounds of self-pity, we should pray for the grace to forgive. Instead of worrying about those for whom we are responsible, we should ask God to intervene and lift the burden from our shoulders. Instead of thinking creatively about how to bring someone else down, we should pray creatively to build them up.

When I lived in England, my landlady had a little wall plaque that read, "Why pray when you can worry?" I always saw the humor of it, and the reverse psychology was good for me. It always drove me to say, "Why worry when you can pray?"

Stressful thoughts create resistance to the joy, happiness, and abundance that we desire. These thoughts include, "I can't, I am too overworked, I worry, I am afraid, I'm unworthy, it will never happen, I'm not smart enough, I'm too old, I'm too young," and so on. These thoughts are downers that constrict us from expecting greater things and living with an attitude of gratitude! So the key is to change the way we think about life, ourselves, and others.

When I was in college, I was on a date. I was driving my 1975 Ford Granada Ghia and my date and I were returning from dinner on a country road in Indiana. All of a sudden, the gas light came on and the car started sputtering. It coughed and wheezed and finally came to a stop about 500 yards from a farmhouse. It was December, and Indiana is plain cold at that time of year.

My date was amazed that I didn't get mad or try to pull the old "I ran out of gas" gag! (I really had run out of gas!) So I said, "You stay here and I will go see if they have any gas on the farm that I can buy from them." I left the car singing St. Paul's words:

> Rejoice in the Lord, always! Again, I say rejoice!
> Rejoice in the Lord, always! Again, I say rejoice!
> Rejoice in the Lord, always! Again, I say rejoice!
>   Rejoice! Rejoice! Again I say rejoice!
>   Rejoice! Rejoice! Again I say rejoice!

When I got to the farmhouse, I was in a very good mood! And, yes, they did have some gas that I purchased. I even got a cup of hot chocolate for my date and me as part of the deal.

Now that might seem like a small thing, but the small things train us for the big things in life. So that when they hit us—and they do hit us—we are ready to rejoice in the Lord, always, to pray and trust that God is in control, and to recognize that God loves us very much even in the darkest of hours.

So an attitude of gratitude defeats worry and anxiety. How? Let's look at number two:

Gratitude employs prayer with thanksgiving to God.

It's one thing to pray, but it is yet another to pray with thanksgiving to God! Research by Yankelovich Partners for the Lutheran Brotherhood (*USA Today* 1999) reveals that people express their thanks in many ways, but there's no better way than thanking God, who is the source of all good things. According to that research, 45 percent of adults express their thanks by praying, 39 percent by being good role models, 36 percent by volunteering and serving others, 35 percent by participating in a place of worship, and 30 percent by giving money to charity.

Yes, an attitude of gratitude employs prayer with thanksgiving to God! It defeats worry and anxiety! And when we live in gratitude, connected to God through prayer, it is amazing how connected we become to others close to us, even though they may be hundreds of miles away.

Many years ago, while I was a student at Duke Divinity School in Durham, North Carolina, I was invited to lead a workshop in Raleigh, North Carolina, on utilizing mass media for promoting God's message. I had been lecturing and coaching for a couple of hours, when, all of a sudden, I sensed that something was wrong with a close family member. This was before the days of cellular phones and the Internet. The only way to confirm my uneasy intuition was to go to my home and wait by the telephone.

I told the event coordinator that I had to conclude my session earlier than planned. I immediately left Raleigh and drove to Roxboro, North Carolina, where I was living at the time. As soon as I arrived, I received news that my mother had suffered a severe heart attack in Tarpon Springs, Florida, the place my parents wintered in at the time.

I believe when all the barnacles are cleared, when the peace treaty is signed with God, when we live with an attitude of gratitude without anxiety and with prayer, our souls and spirits are ready for a full life and to expect greater things.

Yes, an attitude of gratitude defeats worry and anxiety by employing prayer with thanksgiving to God in every situation. I, as well as many others, prayed for my mother over the telephone. She recovered from her heart attack and lived another twenty years. Thanks be to God! When we live with this kind of expectancy, our prayers are more effective.

So, to recap, an attitude of gratitude in an Expect Greater Things champion defeats worry and anxiety, employs prayer with thanksgiving to God for everything, and enjoys God's enduring peace that passes all understanding.

And the peace of God, which transcends all understanding, will guard your hearts and your minds in Christ Jesus" (Philippians 4:7). What does this kind of peace look like? Is it Pollyannaish? Is it naïve? Does it look at life through rose tinted glasses? Is it simplistic? Does it wear blinders to the reality of life? Is it like the ostrich who buries its head in the sand?

The truly spiritual person of faith is not Pollyannaish, naïve, or unrealistic. The Expect Greater Things champion is not simplistic, does not wear blinders, and does not act like an ostrich.

The Expect Greater Things champion understands that the peace of God, which transcends all understanding, is often born out the struggle of the soul with the tough questions of life and God. It is achieved by living life realistically and experiencing the toughness of life and faith that teaches us to expect greater things. It is born out of the courage and faith to follow God and find oneself in the process.

G. K. Chesterton (1884–1936), a prolific author and thinker of his time, who found his answers to the paradoxes and problems of life in the Christian faith, made the following observation about courage (2002, 7–8):

> Courage is almost a contradiction in terms. It means a strong desire to live, taking the form of a readiness to die. 'He that will lose his life, the same shall save it.' Is not a piece of mysticism for saints and heroes. It is a piece of everyday advice for sailors or mountaineers. It might be printed in an alpine guide or drill book. The paradox is the whole principle of courage; even of

quite earthly or quite brutal courage. A man cut off by the sea may save his life if he will risk it on the precipice. He can only get away from death by continually stepping within an inch of it. A soldier surrounded by enemies, if he is to cut his way out, needs to combine a strong desire for living with a strange carelessness about dying. He must not merely cling to life, for then he will be a coward, and will not escape. He must not merely wait for death, for then there will be a suicide, and he will not escape. He must seek his life in a spirit of furious indifference to it; he must desire life like water and yet drink death like wine.

This is the kind of courage that throws caution to the wind. It believes that risk is a positive step toward winning the reward. Mary Pickford, a writer and speaker, must have experienced God's peace through the trial and error in her life. She writes some sage advice: "If at first you don't succeed, relax; you're just like the rest of us."

I believe the amount of peace we experience is directly related to the amount of trust we place in God. It is as simple as that.

Finally, a person living with Expect Greater Things attitude of gratitude looks at life through the lenses of faith, not fear.

St. Paul counsels us thus: "Finally, brothers and sisters, whatever is true, whatever is noble, whatever is right, whatever is pure, whatever is lovely, whatever is admirable, if anything is excellent or praiseworthy, think about such things" (Philippians 4:8). Our focus determines whether we live by faith or by fear!

There is an old legend about three men and their sacks. Each had two sacks, one tied to the front of the person's neck and the other tied behind. When the first man was asked what was in his sacks, he said, "In the sack on my back are all the good things friends and family have done. That way they're hidden from view. In the front sack are all the bad things that have happened to me. Every now and then I stop, open the sack, take the things out, examine them, and think about them." Because he concentrated so much on all the bad stuff, he didn't make much progress in life.

The second man was asked the same question. He replied, "In the front sack are all the good things I've done. I like to see them, so quite often I take them out to show them off to people. The sack at the back? I keep all my mistakes in there and carry them all the time. Sure they're heavy. They slow me down, but, you know, for some reason, I can't put them down."

When the third man was asked about his sacks, he answered, "The sack in front is great. There I keep all the positive thoughts I have about people, all the blessings I've experienced, all the great things other people have done for me. The weight isn't a problem. The sack is like sails of a ship. It keeps me going forward.

"The sack on my back is empty. There's nothing in it. I cut a big hole in its bottom. In there I put all the bad things that I can think about myself or hear about others. They go in one end and out the other, so I am not carrying around any extra weight at all."

The third man is an Expect Greater Things champion! He lives with an attitude of gratitude that defeats worry and anxiety; that employs prayer with thanksgiving to God; that enjoys God's enduring peace; and that looks at life through the lenses of faith, not fear!

In a *U.S. News and World Report* article entitled "Happiness Explained" (Holly J. Morris, August, 26, 2001, 46–54), the following observations were made:

"More than sixty scientists have been given millions of dollars in funding to help humanity find happiness. A popular movement among psychologists called *positive psychology* is an attempt to elevate and focus its research on people's strengths rather than only trying to deal with human weaknesses and problems."

Although the United States' standard of living has increased since WWII, the number of people who regard themselves as happy has not. The *same* article says, "Once income provides basic needs, it doesn't correlate to happiness. Nor does intelligence, prestige, or sunny weather. People grow used to new climates, higher salaries, and better cars. Many years and millions of dollars spent on studying and treating depression have reduced most people's level of sadness, but they are not necessarily happier. Researchers have found that self-esteem, spirituality, family, and good marriages and friendships are key to a happy life, as are hope, meaning, and the discovery and pursuit of the right goals. Even helping others to be happy can "jump-start a process that will lead to stronger relationships, renewed hope, and a general upward spiraling of happiness." Just seeing others doing a good deed results in that heartwarming feeling and influences more people to do the same.

Gratitude is another key ingredient to a happy life. People who frequently practiced thankfulness were "not only more joyful; they were healthier, less stressed, more optimistic, and more likely to help others."

Hope and spirituality work together to provide an important basis for a happy life. "Hope fosters optimism, and faith is, by definition, hope for the future. And the Churchgoing form of faith can be a built-in social network. This is not to say that atheists can't be happy, but it helps explain why so many do find happiness in faith, and why researchers continue to find connections between faith, optimism, and physical health."

So now that we have explored the power of expecting greater things for your life, let's move to the next level in the philosophy. The second trait of a Greater Things champion is a desire to grow deeper, higher, and broader in God's love and grace in all aspects of life.

POINTS TO PONDER

- Being at peace with God is an amazing experience that propels us to accomplish our God-given potential through faith.
- Greater Things champions live with an attitude of gratitude.
- An attitude of gratitude defeats worry and anxiety.
- Rejoice in the Lord, always! Again, I say rejoice!
- The small things train us for the big things in life.
- Greater Things champions live life with courage.

QUESTIONS FOR REFLECTION

- Do I live my life as a Greater Things champion? If so, how?
- In the story of the three men with the sacks, which one represents my life now?
- If it is not the third man in the story, then how can I change my focus so that my life is like that of the third man in the story?

PART TWO

GROW IN GREATER THINGS

CHAPTER 7

GROW IN GREATER THINGS THROUGH THE DISCIPLINES OF PRAYER AND CONFESSION

In Part One of this book we explored the power of Expecting Greater Things and learned that it is a wonderful thing to expect greater things in our lives! It is a powerful thing to read about some of the Expect Greater Things pioneers and how their faith in God has helped advance the faith of millions of people. It is also awesome that the Expect Greater Things challenge can be met by trusting in God to achieve greater things in His glory. It is also encouraging to read stories about how God blesses us with Greater Things opportunities and experiences—for example, the story of Ida and my experience of earning an academic degree while studying in Russia and having an Expect Greater Things meeting with Mikhail Gorbachev.

And it is a sobering reality that the stoppers—of fear, of not having a peace treaty with God, and of not clearing the barnacles on the soul—can truly slow us down to merely existing, when God wants us to thrive. But the best news is that God wants us to succeed in expecting greater things so we can bring glory to Him and reach our full potential. This is experienced by living with gratitude, courage, as well as striving for spiritual growth in greater things in every facet of our lives.

This leads us to Part Two of this book: Growing in Greater Things. Growing in Greater Things goes beyond Expecting Greater Things philosophies. It is a serious call for spiritual growth and commitment. It is a natural next step to the joys of expecting greater things.

Growing in Greater Things is about the power of using our minds, hearts, and souls, as well as our imagination to discern God's path for us in this life in preparation for the life to come. Expecting Greater Things makes us aware of the possibilities of our faith and of the power and significance of that faith in our lives. It helps us to celebrate the ancient disciplines of prayer, meditation, study, confession, worship, giving, serving, simplicity, and community. As we learn and apply these disciplines, we will realize that they act as divine conduits for us to understand and experience something extremely important: God's amazing grace! That is what this chapter will explore: the significant ancient disciplines and the power of God's grace.

Do you remember the wonderful words of Jesus? "I tell you the truth, anyone who has faith in me will do what I have been doing. He will do even greater things than these, because I am going to the Father. And I will do whatever you ask in my name, so that the Son may bring glory to the Father. You may ask me for anything in my name, and I will do it" (John 14:12–14).

Jesus said to the Jews who believed in him, "If you continue in my word, you will be my disciples. Then you will know the truth and the truth shall set you free. . . . If the Son shall set you free, you will be free indeed" (John 8:31, 32, 36).

Growing in Greater Things is about being intent on following God's word and discovering the truth. It is about being intent to be the person that God wants us to be! To Grow in Greater Things is a decision to go deeper and to not only learn about the classic disciplines, but to practice them as well and grow spiritually. But as you will learn in Chapter 8, not only will this affect you spiritually, it will also affect you positively in every facet of your life.

So let's explore how we can grow in greater things as we become champions in living life to God's glory!

GROW IN GREATER THINGS THROUGH THE SPIRITUAL DISCIPLINES OF PRAYER AND CONFESSION

> More things are wrought by prayer than this world dreams of.
> Lord Alfred Tennyson

Golf is one of my favorite sports. I have a friend who called me and wanted to play golf. He said, "The forecast is not good today for our golf game. We better pray for good weather! I want to play golf so badly . . . I can taste it." We laughed and I said, "Tell you what, I am in sales, not management. Let's see what the weather does." The weather cleared up. It was a beautiful afternoon. We played eighteen holes. But by the end of the ninth hole, I said to my friend, "Well, you got your answer to prayer." He said, "What do you mean? You said that you are in sales and not management. I didn't even pray for good weather after that because we need the rain so badly." I laughed, patted him on the shoulder, and pointed to the scorecard. "No, you said you wanted to play golf so bad today! You got a sixty-three for the front nine! Way to go!" We both cracked up. Then I said, "Watch out, prayer is a powerful thing. You have to watch what you pray for . . . you might just get it." As Oscar Wilde said, "When the gods wish to punish us they answer our prayers."

The Bible is full of references to the effectiveness of prayer. Songs and hymns exclaim the significance of prayer. And, I imagine, you can remember times when your prayers were exceedingly fruitful.

The New Testament gives us two predominant models for prayer. The first is what I like to refer to as the Private Office of Prayer. The second is the Corporate/Intercessory Prayer. The former is performed alone. It has its basis in the instructions that Jesus gave his disciples about prayer: "But when you pray, go into your room, close the door and pray to your Father, who is unseen.

Then your Father, who sees what is done in secret, will reward you" (Matthew 6:6).

Through the ages this model of prayer has been practiced, and it can be outlined like this:
1. Establish office hours! When do you want to set aside time to pray?
2. Cultivate your personal relationship with God through prayer:

   Intimate discussions including praise, thanksgiving, requests, and listening for answers.
   Keep a journal of your prayers and their answers, with time and date. You will see that God is conversing with you as your prayers are answered.
   Pray for others, yourself, your community of faith, your community, and the world.

A great teaching about this kind of prayer is found in our Expect Greater Things foundational scripture in John (14:12–14). Read it with the Private Office of Prayer in mind and see how different it appears when read that way:

> I tell you the truth, anyone who has faith in me will do what I have been doing. He will do even greater things than these, because I am going to the Father. And I will do whatever you ask in my name, so that the Son may bring glory to the Father. You may ask me for anything in my name, and I will do it.
> John 14:12–14

Do you regularly set aside time alone with God in prayer? If not, then let me encourage you to do so. You will be amazed at how God moves in your life when you take time to listen and talk to God in prayer. Now, let's unpack this text a little more as it relates to prayer.

This text is not only about expecting greater things through our relationship with God, but it is also about prayer! "I will do whatever you ask in my name. . . . You may ask me for anything in my name, and I will do it."

What are the presuppositions in this teaching from Jesus about prayer? First, he is talking to the faithful. Second, he knows that they are followers who are committed to serving to the glory of God. Third, he wants them to understand that prayer is powerful! Fourth, he knows that they will pray for the right, not selfish, reasons. Fifth, he says that they are to pray in His name. So there is a lot of power-packed teaching about the significance of spiritual growth through prayer.

Here is a personal prayer story that was born out of some "office time" when I was a young Christian. Almost every college freshman wants a car on campus. That is the key to true freedom. I was no exception. My father, however, didn't see things in the same light. So when I asked him to let me buy a car, the answer was quick, firm, and to the point: "No." I remember thinking, "Okay, then I will pray for a car." In the process I forgot that I had to honor my mother and my father. So God would not honor a prayer that broke a commandment. No car appeared. Every time I prayed for a car, the answer was "No." I soon gave up on the idea.

In the spring of my freshman year I was asked if I wanted to serve a small country church in Colburn, Indiana. It was eight miles from campus; I only had to preach on Sundays, and if someone got sick, I was expected to visit that person in the hospital. Plus, they would actually pay me around fifty dollars a week! In today's economy that would be about $250 per week. I accepted the job even though I had no car.

Then I went to my father and told him about the church, the job, and the pay. He said, "Well, now I think it is time we went to look for a car, don't you?" The doors opened not only because I could afford the car, but also because I needed it to do a greater thing with my life to the glory of God. God answers prayer in three ways, "Yes," "No," and "Wait." In this case, the answer moved from No to Wait to Yes!

This is a rather trivial example of the power of prayer; a more serious example is the story of a man I know named Herb, and it illustrates the second form of prayer.

CORPORATE AND INTERCESSORY PRAYER

Herb was a member of my congregation in South Bend, Indiana. He was a fine man with a good heart. His cardiologist told him that his physical heart was dying and that he needed a transplant. He was given four months before his heart gave out. So Herb was put on the transplant list.

Herb and his wife, Jean, came to me one day and asked if we could have a healing service for him at a friend's house. Their friends were members of the congregation as well. I believe in the power of prayer, and I know that God can heal people, so I said, "Absolutely."

I suggested that everyone invited to the healing service read James 5:13–16 from the New Testament prior to the meeting:

> Is any one of you in trouble? He should pray. Is anyone happy? Let him sing songs of praise. Is any one of you sick? He should call the elders of the church to pray over him and anoint him with oil in the name of the Lord. And the prayer offered in faith will make the sick person well; the Lord will raise him up. If he has sinned, he will be forgiven. Therefore confess your sins to each other and pray for each other so that you may be healed. The prayer of a righteous man is powerful and effective.

Fifteen of us gathered at the beautiful home of Bruce and Sandy. There were wonderful refreshments and a spirit of expectancy. Prior to the actual time of prayer I told everyone present that if anyone had any sins that were dragging them down, it was important to pray to the Lord for forgiveness so that they could be in a state of clarity and righteousness (James 5:16) with God. Otherwise, their sins would impede the prayer and healing process.

We all took time to pray in silence. You could almost hear the barnacles from our souls falling onto the lovely carpet. Broken treaties with God were transformed into peace treaties. Some treaties were more detailed than others. But as Romans 3:23 states, "All have sinned and fallen short of the glory of God." So confession was necessary. After all, a man's life was on the line! Literally. So we took the scripture at face value and followed the guidelines.

Grow in Greater Things Through the Disciplines of Prayer and Confession 71

I have a small vat of seldom-used holy oil that was blessed at the Church of the Nativity by a Greek Orthodox priest back in 1978. I used it for the first time on Herb. The time for the prayer service arrived, and I invited Herb to sit on a chair that we had put in the center of the room. Then I invited everyone to draw near and place their hands on Herb's head, shoulders, chest, and arms. I invited each person to pray for Herb and many did. Then I opened the vat, put a dab of oil on my fingers, made the sign of the cross on his forehead, and prayed for the healing of his heart until a replacement heart could be found.

It is important that you understand that those in attendance were regular people, not religious zealots. No, it was a gathering of Expect Greater Things champions who believed in the power of God's promises about prayer and healing. There were physicians, teachers, business executives, mechanics, students, and housewives there.

The evening ended with a time for fellowship with goodies from the kitchen. There were no bolts of lightening, no voices from heaven. Nothing of that sort. Just hugs and handshakes as we left the warmth of a home and headed into the evening chill.

One month passed. Two months passed, three, then four. D-Day. Then five, six, seven, eight, nine, ten . . . fifteen . . . eighteen months passed, and Herb was still alive. His heart had not given out or up. Then came the phone call. "John, they have a match!" Everyone was so excited. But it was a false call. More time passed before the next call, "They have a match!" And they did. And some fourteen years later, Herb is alive and well and lives in Lakeland, Florida, with his wife Jean.

Expect Greater Things! Grow in Greater Things through the power of prayer, confession, and healing, and be amazed at what God can do in your life and in the lives of those you love.

Now you might be asking, "Does it always happen that way?" The answer is not always in that fashion, but I do believe that healing through prayer can occur on levels we don't understand. The physical healing might not occur, but God can heal in ways and places . . . in the nooks and crannies of the soul and the psyche that only the Great Physician knows about. The key is to pray! The key is to trust! The key is to have faith! That is the reason why corporate and intercessory prayer combined with the discipline of confession are so important.

So prayer, both private and corporate, is essential to grow more deeply in your faith so that you can achieve your God-given potential. This is true for us as we pray for our loved ones, our communities of faith, our cities, states, nation, world, and the leaders in each of those places.

My prayers have been most effective when I have been most connected to God in mind, body, and spirit. The times that I have been slowed down by the barnacles of self-will are the times that I have had a hard time praying because I wanted to do it "my way" instead of God's Greater Things way. These times are barren times. They serve, by contrast, as a reminder of what it is to be in a great relationship with God. And yet it is never too late to get back on track; that is why prayer and confession are so important!

I love the story of a mystic who lived in Italy. It was said that she had one-on-one encounters with Jesus Himself. The bishop of the area was charged by the Vatican to check it out. So the bishop met with the mystic. He said, "Is it true that you have meetings with Jesus?" She said, "Yes." The bishop said, "Well, next time you have a meeting, call me afterward. I want you to ask Jesus what the content was of my last confession."

Some time passed and the mystic called the bishop. The bishop met with the woman and asked, "So, you met with Jesus again?" The mystic said, "Yes." The bishop asked, "Pray tell, what was my confession of sins during my last confession to the Lord?" She answered, "The Lord said, 'I don't remember.'"

This story illustrates the significance of prayer and confession. It tells us that God hears our confessions. They fall out of the bottom of the sack on his back because he cut a hole in it when his Son died on the cross for us. That proves God's love for us!

If you have an area in your life that needs attention, talk to a friend or spiritual counselor and ask him or her to pray for you. If you see something that is dragging down your friends spiritually, financially, physically, and emotionally, talk to them. If they won't listen, then pray for them until God opens their hearts, their ears, and their minds. Then watch the equity in the relationship grow through the power and the grace of God.

Who do you need to pray for today? What in your life needs to be addressed for you to lead a more productive life for God, yourself, your family, your church, and community? Think about it.

If you are living with some barnacles right now, pray, confess, ask for forgiveness, and you will find your communication with God and your internal soul much stronger! You will literally grow in Greater Things and find new strength and passion for living.

Another amazing discipline that helps us grow in greater things more deeply is that of study.

POINTS TO PONDER

- Growing in Greater Things is about the power of using our minds, hearts, and souls, as well as our imagination to discern God's path for us.
- Grow in Greater Things through the power of prayer, confession, and healing, and be amazed at what God can do in your life and the lives of those you love.
- The key is to pray! The key is to trust! The key is to have faith!

QUESTIONS FOR REFLECTION

- Who do I need to pray for today? What in my life needs to be addressed for me to lead a more productive life for God, myself, my family, my church, and my community? Think about it.
- Am I living with some barnacles right now? If so, what are they?
- Have I prayed, "Lord, I confess…."
- Have I prayed, "Lord, I ask forgiveness for…."

CHAPTER 8

GROW IN GREATER THINGS THROUGH THE SPIRITUAL DISCIPLINE OF STUDY

"Beware of what you set your mind on for that you will surely become." Ralph Waldo Emerson

Study shapes and influences our mind. If you truly want to be a Greater Things champion and achieve greater things in your life, study is essential.

If we want to grow in greater things, it is important that we become lifelong students and not those who study for a grade. Rather, we should become students who want to study to grow in greater things and reach our full potential as people of faith! In this sense, studying is fun, adventurous, and exciting.

"Man's mind, once stretched by a new idea, never goes back to its original dimensions" (Oliver Wendell Holmes). Another way of saying this is to beware of what you set your mind on, for that you will surely become. Study shapes and influences our mind. Each time I picked up a book I discovered a new insight into life. Then, once I began my travels, I learned to study about the people, culture, economy, religious beliefs, politics, and geography of the areas where I would be traveling. Then I learned that studying is not confined to books or lectures; it can be expanded to studying oneself, family, friends, and other people. In short, to study is truly to be a student of life.

This reminds me of a wonderful quote from James Michener, a consummate student and writer about life. It sums up the joy of living life to the fullest:

> The master in the art of living makes little distinction between his work and his play, his labor and his leisure, his mind and his body, his information and his recreation, his love and his religion. He hardly knows which is which. He simply pursues his vision of excellence whatever he does, leaving for others to decide whether he is working or playing. To him he's always doing both.

The key to true study is to immerse ourselves in life and God, which is also a key to growing in greater things! This is truly where God does an inside job on our hearts and minds. And it happens through His grace.

"Inner righteousness is a gift from God to be graciously received. This needed change within us is God's work, not ours. The demand is for an inside job, and only God can work from the inside. In this regard it would be proper for us to speak of the way of disciplined grace. It is 'grace' because it is free; it is 'disciplined' because there is something for us to do" (Dietrich Bonhoeffer). In *The Cost of Discipleship*, Dietrich Bonhoeffer made clear that grace is free, but it is not cheap. Once we clearly understand that God's grace is unearned and unearnable, and if we expect to grow, we must take up a consciously chosen course of action involving both individual and group life. That is the purpose of the spiritual disciplines" (Richard Foster).

So being a student of life and love leads us to the inner workings of grace so that we may grow into God's purpose for us. As students of life our mind expands, and we believe that we can expect, grow, and do greater things to the glory of God as champions of faith. When we start to see things in this light, our life takes on a larger purpose and scope. We begin to thrive on far horizons.

So study is essential for us to grow in greater things. It is so important that I want to give you some tips to study in such a way that you can truly grow as a Greater Things champion in order to fulfill your God-given destiny.

There are many excellent books, but the best-selling book in history is the Bible. I like to call it the Greater Things Handbook for Life!

But how can we best understand the Handbook? There are four steps that I like to utilize as I study the Bible. These can be added to your Private Office Time, and they are repetition, concentration, comprehension, and reflection.

Repetition. Repetition is a way of regularly channeling the mind in a specific direction, thus ingraining habits of thought. In psychocybernetics we are taught to send ourselves positive messages so that our mind will start to assimilate them into our subconscious, and eventually our subconscious will make the statement a reality. In this case a message like "I want to be thin . . . I am thin . . ." could help an overweight person work toward the goal of better health.

Another example from Hollywood is the movie *Caddyshack,* in which Chevy Chase's character is always chanting, "Be the Ball . . . nanananananana . . . nananananana . . . nanananananana. . . Be the ball." I always laugh at that scene!

And yet, as unproven as those two examples might seem, repetition has been part of studying and learning for centuries. The monks of medieval times used to recite mantras. And some places of worship today still do so as a means of study, meditation, and prayer.

I learned a great deal about this during my two-year tenure at the Academy for Spiritual Formation in Nashville, Tennessee. We were taught the importance of repetition in study and prayer. My mantra was "Lord, help me be gentle." Now I am a teddy bear!

I also use repetition when I am studying something that I want to learn. This is true whether it's lyrics of a song, a passage of Scripture, or a quote from a book. Repeating things helps me assimilate them into my mind.

Concentration. Concentration centers the mind and gets rid of distractions. While writing this book I have shut myself off from almost all distractions. The phone is turned down, and the only sound in my study is that of classical music. This way I am able to think, reflect, and dig into my deeper psyche and spirit to sense the direction that God wants me to take in the writing process. And, as I concentrate, I am amazed at the number of stories that come to the surface of my consciousness. For the record, even though I love classical music, I usually listen to a wide variety of music, from country to top forty.

Concentration helps me to remember the names of people. It helps me focus on the tasks at hand and memorize the Scripture and other important information.

Comprehension. Comprehension leads to insight and discernment. It provides the basis for true insight into reality.

Sometimes college students practice repetition and concentration as they prepare for exams. They pass them sometimes with a perfect score without comprehending what they had studied. After the exam, it is as if they do a brain-dump. The result might be a great grade point average, but without the substance to back it up when life requires it.

If we are to grow in greater things, it is essential that we employ repetition, concentration, and comprehension. This is what Jesus was talking about when he said, "If you continue in my Word, then you will be my disciples and you shall know the truth!" (John 8:32). Comprehension gives us insights into the truth that comes from study.

Reflection. Although comprehension defines what we are studying, reflection defines the significance of it. This is where the "Aha!" moments arise. It is in this fourth part of study that we understand "you will know the truth and the truth shall set you free!"

This is where knowledge gained from repetition, concentration, and comprehension is transformed by imagination that has, in turn, been ignited by reflection. And this is where ideas are born. Our imagination creates ideas that change our souls and the course of life and history.

> Imagination is not the talent of some men, but is the health of every man. Ralph Waldo Emerson

If you take the time to practice these four steps in your study and devotional life, you will know true joy. And you will have knowledge and understanding to treasure for the rest of your life.

The American Bible Society has a wonderful study tool called PRESS (pray, read, examine, summarize, share) to help people learn the Bible.

QUIET TIMES WITH GOD . . . FROM THE COACHING CENTER

Every day, set aside a special time called *Quiet Time*. During this time you can talk to God and let Him talk to you through the Bible. There are a lot of good methods that can be used for your Quiet Time. PRESS is one such method.

1. *Pray*

   Begin by thanking God for the new day, and then ask Him to help you learn from what you read.

2. *Read*

   To get started, read the following verses on the designated days:

   Day 1 Luke 19:1–9
   Day 2 Luke 9:23–26
   Day 3 Hebrews 10:19–25
   Day 4 Ecclesiastes 4
   Day 5 Keep going! Start reading the Gospel of John.

3. *Examine*

   Ask yourself the following questions: What is the main point of this passage? What does it tell me about God? About myself?

4. *Summarize*

   Do one of the following:

   Rewrite the verses in your own words.
   Outline what each verse is saying.
   Give each verse a one-word title which summarizes it.

5. *Share*

   Talk with God about what you've learned. Also, take time each day to share with someone you know what you learned in your Quiet Time.

   Having a daily Quiet Time is extremely important. It is the key to developing spiritually. You might want to continue your Quiet Time by reading in the book of Mark or John. Choose a few verses each day and use the PRESS method

(American Bible Society). Thanks to the American Bible Society for creating this valuable tool.

So, as you can see, the spiritual discipline of being a student of life can help you grow to heights you never thought possible. Without study my life would be substantially different. It would be one or two dimensional at best in terms of my spirituality and faith.

The disciplines of prayer, confession, and study have changed my life. I truly don't know whether I am working or playing. It is all good! I encourage you to commit to these disciplines, if you haven't done so already.

In the next chapter, utilizing everything we have learned thus far in the book, we will explore six areas where we can grow in greater things more deeply. These areas are:

> Grow in Greater Things Spiritually
> Grow in Greater Things Relationally
> Grow in Greater Things Financially

POINTS TO PONDER

- If you truly want to be a Greater Things champion and achieve greater things in your life, study is essential.
- Being a student of life is fun, adventurous, and exciting.
- Studying is not confined to books or lectures; it can be expanded to studying oneself, family, friends, and other people and cultures.
- True study is to immerse ourselves in life and God.

QUESTIONS FOR REFLECTION

- Do I have a time set aside each day for study, reflection, and prayer? If not, what can I do to establish one and follow the guidelines in this chapter?
- When was the most enjoyable time of learning and spiritual growth in my life? What made it so significant for me?
- What can I do today to begin deepening my study of myself, others, and God?

CHAPTER 9

THREE KEY AREAS TO GROW IN GREATER THINGS

Grow in Greater Things Spiritually
Grow in Greater Things Relationally
Grow in Greater Things Financially

GROW IN GREATER THINGS SPIRITUALLY

Once we get to the point of developing a healthy imagination through prayer, study, and confession, we will begin to see life differently. We will look at life through spiritual lenses. As our spirituality deepens, we will gain a greater vision of God's purpose for us. And once we are empowered with a vision, we will feel joy in traversing and fulfilling our journeys. But earning a vision is not always easy. It takes planning, focus, and commitment.

It is important to have a vision for our life, our family, our faith community, our career, our company, our nation, and our role in all of them. One of my favorite passages in the book of Proverbs tells us, "Where there is no vision, the people perish" (29:18). That is telling us that vision is extremely important. Look at that again: "Where there is no vision, the people perish."

But how do we gain a vision? I think you will be surprised that it doesn't come out of thin air. In fact, a vision is born out of a process.

Another translation of the same verse from the New King James version of the Bible says, "Where there is no revelation, the people cast off restraint" (Proverbs 29.18).

How do we get revelations? Often some of my most telling ideas come out of my prayer time, my studies, and my experience of life! Sometimes they come after a good night's sleep!

One such revelation occurred the day we met with Mikhail Gorbachev. I awoke thinking "We should ask him about his spirituality. We should ask him if he has any faith. We should ask him if he would like to pray with us." Over breakfast I brought this up with the leaders of the group. They said that that was an important series of questions. We finally met the former leader of the Communist Soviet Union, an avowed atheist. But in our conversation he spoke of being baptized and of the importance of spirituality and the inner soul. And he accepted our invitation to pray together.

This wasn't a huge vision, but it was an important one that led us to some important discussions with and insights on one of twentieth century's most significant leaders.

Another vision I gained was before I was sent to a church in South Bend, Indiana. At the time, I was an associate pastor in a downtown church in Fort Wayne, Indiana. I had been there just over four years and really wanted a church of my own. I prayed about it and wrote in my journal that I believed God was going to send me to a church in the suburbs with lots of families and opportunities for growth.

Some months later I took my youth group on a ski trip to southern Michigan, just over the state line near South Bend. I had to attend the funeral of a friend in South Bend that day, so my counselors took the kids skiing and then to the mall. On my way to meet the group, I passed a United Methodist church that was situated on seven acres of land. It wasn't a very well developed piece of property, and the church looked a little weary. I pulled into the parking lot and sat there for a few minutes. And, no kidding, in those few minutes, I had a vision of what was going to happen at that church. The vision did not appear in an eerie way, but in a matter-of-fact "this is going to happen" way.

I decided not to tell anyone about it. So I wrote about it in my journal. Six months later my superior called and said that I was going to be sent to that exact church. I wasn't surprised! My vision for that congregation came to pass. We grew from eighty-one to over seven-hundred in worship. We expanded the parking lot three times, built three buildings, and created ministries to reach inner-city children. We even had a staff member in Russia.

As the years rolled by, I had another vision to buy thirty-five acres and build a second campus. But the people weren't ready to do that. I moved to Florida to pursue other opportunities, but seven years later, the church in South Bend continued to grow and they bought the acreage. They have built the second campus!

Sometimes we can gain a vision and see it come to fruition. Other times we may gain a vision and see others bring it to fruition. But the good news is that both visions are important and valid. *Where there is a vision, the people will flourish!*

The process of vision . . .

> Starts with a heart in prayer
>
> Evaluates resources under one's care
>
> And studies from there
>
> Then networks and shares
>
> It is owned by those who care
>
> Then it is broadcast from there

Vision Starts with a Heart in Prayer. If you want to experience the spark of vision and what God has in store for you as a person of faith, spend time in prayer. It is here that you will get an idea of what God has in mind for your life and what greater things He wants you to do and be!

Evaluates Resources Under One's Care. Once we gain a vision of God's purpose for us, we are to take stock of our resources. For instance, if you have a vision for starting a new business, look at your available resources of time, skill set, funds, intellectual capital, personnel, and so on.

And Studies from There. Is this a great idea? Is anyone else doing it? If not, why not? If so, should I duplicate it? Whose help do I need to make the vision a reality? Why is this important for people to respond to it? Where will I make the vision a reality? What is the timeline? What materials are available for me to study? Who can counsel me to fulfill the vision with excellence?

Then Networks and Shares. Who can I talk to about the vision after I have done my homework? Who might want to help me make the vision a reality? What will people that I respect say about the vision? What can I learn from their responses?

It is Owned by Those Who Care. By the time you get to this stage, you know that the vision is on its way to becoming reality! You have a team committed to working together and the vision guiding them with the courage to make it happen. At this stage, you are ready to relate your vision to others and tell them how it will positively impact the lives of people.

Then It is Broadcast from There. Once you have the vision and a plan to work it into reality, you are ready to go public! This can be exciting and scary at the same time. Some will agree with your vision. Others may not! Some will pat you on the back. Others will talk behind your back. Some may celebrate your courage. Others may envy you and try to defeat you. But the bottom line is this: If God gave you the vision and if you have reached this point, both the praise and gossip don't matter all that much. They are simply noise, positive and negative, that accompanies a great vision.

Being a person of faith leads one to becoming a person of vision! So why not have huge visions for your life? Why not dream big dreams and thrive in them? Why not say, "I can do greater things with my life to the glory of God and the betterment of others?" I love what Oliver Wendell Holmes said: "No person who thinks in terms of catching mice will ever catch lions."

I want to ask you a question. What is your vision for life? What is it that you most desire to do? What is it that you believe God is nudging you to think about during your prayer and study time? If there was one thing that you could achieve in five years, what would it be? Are you a mouse catcher or a lion tamer? Go for the lions! It takes guts! It takes courage! It takes faith in God and yourself! But the rewards are amazing.

President Theodore Roosevelt, in speaking about achievement through vision, blood, sweat, and tears, wrote: "It is not the critic who counts; not the man or woman who points out how the strong man stumbled, or where the doer of deeds could have done them better. The credit belongs to the man who is actually in the arena, whose face is marred by dust and sweat and blood; who strives valiantly; who errs and comes short again and again; who knows the great enthusiasms, the great devotions; who spends himself in a worthy cause; who, at the best, knows in the end the triumph of high achievement, and who, at the worst, if he fails, at least fails while daring greatly, so that his place shall never be with those timid souls who know neither victory or defeat."

So how about it? Are you ready to catch the vision? Or perhaps you are in the middle of exercising your God-given vision! That is excellent. Below are some questions that might help in forming or clarifying your vision. You can pray about it and write down your answers in the next few days.

Five-Year Strategic Visionary Planning:

- Where do you see God leading you in five years?
- What do you want to accomplish?
- Who do you want to be?
- What do you want to do?
- How do you plan to leverage your life and life's force to bring glory to God and to help others?

You can also write vision statements for different areas of your life. Here are a few of my vision statements:

Personal Vision Statement

I want to provide exemplary visionary leadership that will inspire, influence, and motivate individuals, families, organizations, universities, and corporations reach their full spiritual, material, and philanthropic potential in order to make a systemic impact in the world. This will be achieved as I strive to be a person of prayer, study, health, and balance.

Family

It is my vision to empower my family members with love, guidance, and resources to help them achieve their visions. I want to celebrate their families as they grow. Additionally, I want my family to thrive in love for one another and in serving God through their skills and passion for life.

Business

Greater Things Enterprises' vision is to focus on faith development, spiritual formation, leadership, ethics, values, and relationship equity in the home, faith community, classroom, and boardroom. The vision is to provide a significant one-stop shop on the Internet and to celebrate Greater Things champions on radio, television, the Internet, and through publications.

Communities of Faith

My vision statement in this regard, which is also the vision statement of the First United Methodist Church of Jupiter/Tequesta, is to make disciples of Jesus Christ to the glory of God with passion and excellence in all things.

Having a vision statement for each area of your life can stretch you beyond the status quo. As Goethe said, "If you treat an individual as he is, he will stay that way, but if you treat him as if he were what he could be, he will become what he could be." *Where there is a vision, the people flourish!*

TRANSFORMATIONAL PRAYER

Dear God, thank you for giving us the gift of vision and the opportunity for transformation! Help us to live our lives to the fullest.

Forgive us when we live by fear and doubt instead of faith and sustained vision.

Set our hearts and minds on living expectantly by Your power. Amen.

POINTS TO PONDER

- Grow in Greater Things spiritually.
- Earning a vision is not always easy. It takes planning, focus, and commitment.
- The process of vision . . .

  Starts with a heart in prayer

  Evaluates resources under one's care

  And studies from there

  Then networks and shares

  It is owned by those who care

  Then it is broadcast from there

QUESTIONS FOR REFLECTION

- Do I have a five-year strategic visionary plan that addresses the questions:

  Where do I see God leading me in five years?

  What do I want to accomplish?

  Who do I want to be?

  What do I want to do?

  How do I plan to leverage my life and life's force to bring glory to God and to help others?

- Have I begun work on this plan by writing my vision statements for:

  my personal vision?

  my family vision?

  my business/professional/career/work vision?

  my faith vision?

  my recreational vision?

GROW IN GREATER THINGS RELATIONALLY

Relationship Equity that Expects Greater Things

Years ago someone asked me to list my favorite top-ten sermons that I had heard. I struggled to come up with three or four. Then they asked me to list the winners of the last ten Super Bowls, and I came up with a few.

Then they asked me to tell them about the top-ten people who have influenced my life! That list was easy to create! In fact, there were many more than ten people in it.

Relationship equity adds value to your life! It spans the years and helps you live life to the fullest! Relationships count! The book of Proverbs gives us some great insights to healthy and growing relationships.

Proverbs 27

27:5 Better is open rebuke than hidden love.

27:6 Wounds from a friend can be trusted, but an enemy multiplies kisses.

27:7 He who is full loathes honey, but to the hungry even what is bitter tastes sweet.

27:8 Like a bird that strays from its nest is a man who strays from his home.

27:9 Perfume and incense bring joy to the heart, and the pleasantness of one's friend springs from his earnest counsel.

Proverbs 27 contains one of my favorite messages about the importance of true friendship. It says that a friend is someone who will sit you down and tell you like it is. We might not like what we hear, but we would be wise to give it consideration.

If something in your life needs attention, talk to a friend or spiritual counselor, and ask him or her to pray for you. If you see something in your friends' lives that is dragging them down spiritually, financially, physically, or emotionally, talk to them. If they won't listen, then pray for them until God opens their hearts, their ears, and their minds. Then watch the equity in the relationship grow through the power and the grace of God.

The value of relationship equity is a two-way street that changes our lives. If we have positive and truthful relationships, our lives are the better for it. I will give you a case in point from my own life. I don't know about you, but I have always struggled with yo-yo up-and-down weight control. At the time of the writing of this book, I am forty pounds lighter than my heaviest weight. But, I am several pounds heavier than a healthy weight. Those who are my most precious friends and family members have most recently shared their concerns. In fact, their messages are so similar that I am hearing it as a larger message from God's spirit.

Some have even given me incentives like new clothes when I reach my goals and objectives nutritionally and physically. Another (while I was staying at their home as a guest) hired a Christian massage therapist who gave me an amazing massage and prayed over me in the process.

Because of their "open rebuke" instead of their "hidden love," I am changing my lifestyle and eating behaviors. In fact, I am considering writing a book entitled, *Expect Greater Things by Losing the Weight*. But this book would be holistic in its approach. It will deal with losing weight and getting in shape. It will deal with losing unhealthy eating and drinking behaviors. It will also deal with losing the weight of stress, guilt, debt, and other things that weigh us down. But I can't write it with integrity until I have the results that I want, my friends and family want, and that (I believe) God wants.

The point is this: our relationship equity will always seek to advance us in our lives personally, spiritually, relationally, physically, financially, and philanthropically.

Who do you need to pray for today? What in your life needs to be addressed for you to lead a more productive life for God, yourself, your family, your church, and your community? Think about it!

The power of relationship equity is also great for advancing your visions and desires. The Psalmist writes, "Delight yourself in the Lord and He will give you the desires of your heart. Commit your way to the Lord; trust in Him and He will do this: He will make your righteousness shine like the dawn, the justice of your cause like the noonday sun" (Psalm 37:4–6).

When we have enough faith to find delight and happiness in our relationship with God, then our hearts' desires are in line with God's will. As a result, the right people appear at the right time to help us make our dreams and visions realities. And, at times, when we think someone is right when they are not, circumstances will occur that will direct our paths away from those who appear as angels of light. There are some people who delight in appearing to help us achieve our goals, objectives, and visions, but only for selfish gain. In time, they are found out by the support of trusted equity relationships that have been in place for a very long time. When we commit ourselves to expecting greater things, growing in greater things, and doing greater things, it is amazing how the doors open for us. And, it is equally amazing how the doors sometimes close for us.

In the midst of it all, God brings friends, associates, acquaintances, family members, and a host of others to support, guide, contribute, and participate in our enterprises and lives. And sometimes we are directed to help others achieve greater things as well. That's because relationships are two-way streets that span the years.

My first full time assignment in a church was as an associate pastor. I was twenty-six and I worked with Virgil, one of the finest men I have known. He was my boss and mentor, and I was fortunate to work with him for three years before he retired. But we maintained our friendship for over twenty-two years. He was a wise soul.

I received an unexpected phone call from Virgil in January 2004. He said, "John, this is Virg. I want you to know that I am calling nine people, and you are the first. You know I have been on dialysis. Well, I am tired of it. And I am ready to go home to God and to see Frannie [his wife who passed away several years before]. I am calling you to tell you good bye. I am calling to tell you that I love you. I am calling to tell you that I am proud of you." My throat had swollen up a bit at this point. I said, "I am honored that you are calling. Is there anything I can do?" He said, "Just pray and continue your work with excellence."

The next morning I was on a jet bound from Fort Lauderdale, Florida, to Indianapolis, Indiana. By evening, I made it to the

Assisted Living Facility in Fort Wayne. I walked in and saw his daughters and sons-in-law. I said, "I wanted to surprise him. Can you see if I can go in to say hi?" They came out and said, "You have been granted an audience." We all laughed.

My visit with Virgil was amazing. We laughed as we shared memories. There were no tears. Virgil was ready to go home. He was at peace, complete peace, and excited to go on the final journey. And I was honored to be the first person that he called before then. He was a class act, and even as he prepared for death, he continued to mentor me.

He also taught me to value the healthy relationships in my life and not take them for granted; he taught me to stay in touch with them despite the distance. So I make it a point to do so with my friends and family. And, from time to time, I remember to say, "Thank you for being my friend."

This is not a new sentiment. Albert Schweitzer had already written about it.

> When I look back upon my early days, I am stirred by the thought of the number of people whom I have to thank for what they gave me or what they were to me. At the same time, I am haunted by an oppressive consciousness of the little gratitude I really showed them while I was young. How many of them have said farewell to life without my having made clear to them what it meant to me to receive from them so much kindness or so much care. Many a time have I, with a feeling of shame, said quietly to myself over a grave the words which my mouth ought to have spoken to the departed, while he was still in the flesh.

Growing in greater things relationally means that we intentionally cultivate, cherish, grow, and invest in the lives of others. It means having healthy relationships that advance our lives in every way. And it means understanding that we are not static, that we grow and develop. Writing these lines brings to mind a story about Mahatma Gandhi.

One day a disillusioned follower of Mahatma Gandhi asked him, "You have no integrity. Last week I heard you say one thing, and today you are saying something different. How do you justify such vacillation?"

Gandhi quietly replied, "It is simple, really, my son. I have learned something since last week."

A good friend celebrates your new learning and makes room for personal growth. An unhealthy friend would be jealous of it because it might alter the friendship and upset the status quo. Strong, healthy Greater Things friendships celebrate growth, new opportunities, and possibilities. They want you to succeed so that they can celebrate with you. A truly healthy friend realizes that all boats rise with the tide!

So, today, check out your relationships. Are they healthy? Are they balanced? Do they advance your visions? Do you advance theirs? Surround yourself with excellent people, and your life will be qualitatively different and effective. You can either soar with the eagles or run with the turkeys! It is your choice. Choose the eagles!

POINTS TO PONDER

- Relationship equity builds an Expect Greater Things lifestyle.
- Relationship equity adds value to your life! It spans the years and helps you live life to the fullest!
- Relationships count!
- If something in your life needs attention, talk to a friend or spiritual counselor, and ask him or her to pray for you.
- The power of relationship equity is great for advancing your visions and desires.
- Surround yourself with excellent people, and your life will be qualitatively different and effective.

> **QUESTIONS FOR REFLECTION**
> - Whom do you need to pray for today?
> - What in your life needs to be addressed for you to lead a more productive life . . .
>   for God?
>   yourself?
>   your family?
>   your church?
>   and your community?
> - What is your plan to develop positive relationship equity in your life?
> - Are your relationships healthy?
> - Are they balanced?
> - Do they advance your visions?
> - Do you advance theirs?

GROW IN GREATER THINGS FINANCIALLY

Growing in Greater Things financially happens as we expand and deepen our hearts, minds, souls, and practical skills of wealth management as it relates to God's abundance. As we train our minds for Growing in Greater Things and learn to see beyond the everyday, many financial opportunities will reveal themselves to us! But what perspective do we need to be a Greater Things champion when it comes to our material goods and possessions? The following might give us some insight.

Did you know that the Bible has approximately 500 verses on prayer, less than that on faith, but approximately 2,350 verses on managing our possessions and wealth? Is prayer important? Absolutely! Is faith important? Absolutely! And yet the Bible contains four times more teaching on managing God's resources than it does on prayer and faith! Wow!

So we don't want to miss these teachings, do we? I remember taking a class once on perspectives of food and world hunger. For an entire semester all we did was study the abundance of food produced worldwide and the degree of starvation that still persisted despite that abundance. It was amazingly sad. And it all came down to how corporations, governments, individuals, and societies manage their resources. Much of it came down to politics and economics. But the most astonishing fact is the abundance of wealth that we all have if only we learn to see it and manage it properly.

John Wesley had a great philosophy on wealth management. He said, "Gain all you can. Save all you can. Give all you can." And John D. Rockefeller believed in giving ten percent of everything he had. He said, "I never would have been able to get the first million dollars I ever made if I hadn't tithed my first salary, which was $1.50 a week." He learned the principles of Greater Things wealth management early in his life.

Jesus said, "Do not store up for yourselves treasures on earth, where moth and rust destroy, and where thieves break in and steal. But store up for yourselves treasures in heaven, where moth and rust do not destroy, and where thieves do not break in and steal. For where your treasure is, there your heart will be also" (Matthew 6:19–21).

It is all about perspective and the way we train our minds to think about material things. Martin Luther, the great reformer, said there were three necessary things for a person to live a full and abundant life of faith. They were (1) the conversion of the heart; (2) the conversion of the mind; (3) and the conversion of the wallet. Richard Foster, in *Money, Sex and Power*, tells us that, of these three, he found the conversion of the wallet to be the most difficult.

The prophet Malachi in the Old Testament wrote, "'Bring the whole tithe into the storehouse, that there may be food in my house. Test me in this,' says the Lord Almighty, 'and see if I will not throw open the floodgates of heaven and pour out so much blessing that you will not have room enough for it'" (3:10). Wow, what a promise! It is a message that the person who is Growing in Greater Things financially, with wealth management, will thrive in this life. It is entrepreneurial of God to say to us, "Test me in this."

But how do we gain the faith to actually test God in this principle? It all has to do with our perspective. A great friend of mine, Mr. Mark Moehlman, from Newport Beach, California, has a company called the Wealth Management Network. He and his wife are true Greater Things champions. I met Mark on one of my trips to Russia, and we became fast friends.

Mark, who also uses the *nom de plume* Robin Hood, wrote the following poem about his work. It illustrates the idea of Greater Things wealth management that ultimately benefits the larger community as well as the self.

The Wealth Manager

His nickname was Robin Hood;
He did well by doing good.
He was blind to your color, deaf to your creed;
Focusing only on your wealth management needs!

He counseled the rich to share with the poor;
Teaching that less could often mean more.
After an hour in his presence, you clearly would see
That one key to happiness is philanthropy.

He delighted in serving as a financial guide,
Ultimately insisting you swallow your pride.
After all, he asserted, you're born with no wealth,
And all's left behind when you run out of health!

Ponder this profound thought as you try to decide
Whom to trust . . . and from whom to hide:
If you bring nothing into this world and take nothing out,
Then what's all the worry over money about?

What most people seek is peace of mind,
A transformation, he believed, of the spiritual kind.
He prayed that all would understand, when they heard him say,
That you simply can't keep what you won't give away!

Mark and I created the following common sense principles (Wealth Management Network and Greater Things Enterprises 2000).

TEN GREATER THINGS PRINCIPLES OF WEALTH MANAGEMENT

1. We bring nothing into this world, and we take nothing out of this world.
2. All wealth is God's; we are but temporary stewards of whatever we control and create.
3. If we think we own something, then it really owns us.
4. The more we give, the more we get.
5. The true measure of success is what we do with what we get.
6. It is not a sin to be "wealthy"; neither is it a virtue.
7. We are all philanthropists, whether by design or by default.
8. If we think we're rich, or think we're poor, we're right.
9. Never make a financial decision while feeling pressured to do so.
10. If your outgo exceeds your income, your upkeep has become your downfall.

If you want to delve deeper into financial and material wealth management, please visit www.expectgreaterthings.com. There are tools there to help you grow in greater things financially.

POINTS TO PONDER

- The Bible contains four times more teaching on managing God's resources than it does on prayer and faith.
- "Gain all you can. Save all you can. Give all you can." John Wesley

QUESTIONS FOR REFLECTION

- How do the ten principles for wealth management apply to my life?
- Am I balanced and healthy or do I need to reflect and do a tune up?
- What exactly should I do in order to grow in greater things financially?

PART THREE

DO GREATER THINGS

CHAPTER 10

DO GREATER THINGS

To Do Greater Things is to have compassion for people and be committed to helping them not with a hand out, but with a hand up! Martin Luther King Jr. wrote,

> The well-off and the secure have too often become indifferent and oblivious to the poverty and the deprivation in their midst. The poor have been shut out of our minds and driven from the mainstream of our societies, because we have allowed them to become invisible. Ultimately, a great nation is a compassionate nation. No nation can be great if it does not have a concern for "the least of these."

What does it mean to Do Greater Things?

> By this we know love, because He laid down His life for us. And we also ought to lay down our lives for the brethren. But whoever has this world's goods, and sees his brother in need, and shuts up his heart from him, how does the love of God abide in him? My little children, let us not love in word or in tongue, but in deed and in truth. 1 John 3:16–18

To Do Greater Things is to put our faith into action. It is to fulfill the word of Jesus that we will Do Greater Things. It is to live with the confidence that we can do all things through our faith in God who provides us with strength as we expect greater things and grow in greater things. It is to remember Jesus' teaching that when we have cared for the homeless, the imprisoned, the hungry, the naked, the stranger, and the sick, that we have cared for Jesus Himself (Matthew 25).

Doing Greater Things is what psychologist Abraham Maslow termed self-actualization. It is what Mother Teresa called being faithful. She said, "God does not call us to be successful. God calls us to be faithful." In that faithfulness we do greater things and impact the culture in which we live.

Doing Greater Things is what the spiritual entrepreneur John Wesley termed, "social holiness." Wesley believed in grace, justification, assurance, and sanctification. He combined those beliefs in a powerful and distinctive manner to emphasize living the full life of faith.

Doing Greater Things is where faith meets life!

Wesley and those who ascribe to his theology today

> insist that personal salvation always involves Christian mission and service to the world. By joining heart and hand, we assert that personal religion, evangelical witness, and Christian social action are reciprocal and mutually reinforcing.

In other words, a vital spirituality requires faith in God, a passion to share that faith with others, and a determination to Do Greater Things. What are some practical applications that illustrate doing greater things? Doing greater things is not to be narrowly defined. In fact, doing greater things has broad applications.

Doing greater things occurs after we have mastered the art of living. It occurs when we understand that all wealth belongs to God and that we are temporary stewards of it. In following that philosophy, we won't feel the need to "control" everything. We won't worry about tomorrow because we are living in the present. We trust God for the day at hand and for the days to follow, and we commit our daily schedules and activities to expecting greater things as we live in faith. We commit ourselves to growing in greater things so that we can truly deepen our lives spiritually, intellectually, financially, and relationally. As we grow in greater things, we discover that we have a vision to do greater things, and that we are moving from struggle to success to significance and to self actualization. The movement is wonderful! It is amazing! Life takes on a whole new dimension, one in which we no longer live for ourselves, but for God and for others. This process prepares us to Do Greater Things to the glory of God.

But arriving at this point in our lives isn't always easy or simple. Sometimes it involves pain. One of my favorite stories that illustrates this point occurs in the following in *The Velveteen Rabbit*.

> For a long time he lived in the toy cupboard or on the nursery floor, and no one thought very much about him. He was naturally shy, and being only made of velveteen, some of the more expensive toys quite snubbed him. The mechanical toys were very superior, and looked down upon every one else; they were full of modern ideas, and pretended they were real. The model boat, who had lived through two seasons and lost most of his paint, caught the tone from them and never missed an opportunity of referring to his rigging in technical terms. The Rabbit could not claim to be a model of anything, for he didn't know that real rabbits existed; he thought they were all stuffed with sawdust like himself, and he understood that sawdust was quite out-of-date and should never be mentioned in modern circles. Even Timothy, the jointed wooden lion, who was made by the disabled soldiers, and should have had broader views, put on airs and pretended he was connected with Government. Between them all the poor little Rabbit was made to feel himself very insignificant and commonplace, and the only person who was kind to him at all was the Skin Horse.
>
> The Skin Horse had lived longer in the nursery than any of the others. He was so old that his brown coat was bald in patches and showed the seams underneath, and most of the hairs in his tail had been pulled out to string bead necklaces. He was

wise, for he had seen a long succession of mechanical toys arrive to boast and swagger, and by-and-by break their mainsprings and pass away, and he knew that they were only toys, and would never turn into anything else. For nursery magic is very strange and wonderful, and only those playthings that are old and wise and experienced like the Skin Horse understand all about it.

"What is REAL?" asked the Rabbit one day, when they were lying side by side near the nursery fender, before Nana came to tidy the room. "Does it mean having things that buzz inside you and a stick-out handle?"

"Real isn't how you are made," said the Skin Horse. "It's a thing that happens to you. When a child loves you for a long, long time, not just to play with, but REALLY loves you, then you become Real."

"Does it hurt?" asked the Rabbit.

"Sometimes," said the Skin Horse, for he was always truthful. "When you are Real you don't mind being hurt."

"Does it happen all at once, like being wound up," he asked, "or bit by bit?

"It doesn't happen all at once," said the Skin Horse. "You become. It takes a long time. That's why it doesn't happen often to people who break easily, or have sharp edges, or who have to be carefully kept. Generally, by the time you are Real, most of your hair has been loved off, and your eyes drop out and you get loose in the joints and very shabby. But these things don't matter at all, because once you are Real you can't be ugly, except to people who don't understand."

Doing greater things is about being real! It is taking life by the horns and deciding to utilize life's experiences, passions, failures, expectations, skills, resources, and abilities to make a difference in the lives of others. Taking life by the horns is essential for a passionate life that makes a difference. And the best way to take life by the horns is to live life to the fullest so that we know what the horns look like!

I love the following story. The Monday Afternoon Club, an organization of wealthy city women, met and decided that the month's outing was to be at a dairy farm. Most of them had lived in the city all their lives, and they had never seen such a thing. The day came, and the ladies filed into the rented bus that whisked them off to their destination. On the way, they watched city squalor turn into lovely, unpolluted countryside.

After they arrived, they were greeted by the farmer who invited them to ask questions, should they have any. Myrtle, after looking around in amazement, stepped into a building and viewed something she thought was quite remarkable. She saw the farmer walk by and hailed him; he sauntered in. "Sir," she inquired, "Why doesn't this cow have any horns?"

The farmer cocked his head for a moment, then explained patiently: "Well, ma'am, cattle can do a powerful lot of damage with horns. Sometimes we keep 'em trimmed down with a hacksaw. Other times we can fix up the young 'uns by puttin' a couple drops of acid where their horns would grow in, and that stops 'em cold. Still, there are some breeds of cattle that never grow horns. But the reason this cow don't have no horns, ma'am, is 'cause it's a horse."

Yes, experience is a great teacher; it helps us identify how to take life by the horns by identifying true needs and then stepping up to the plate to do something great for God and for other people.

The remainder of this book will touch on several ways to do greater things with your life! This is where we find significance in living.

Do Greater Things through Generosity
Do Greater Things for Your Community
Do Greater Things Environmentally
Do Greater Things Through a Lasting Legacy

POINTS TO PONDER

- To Do Greater Things is to have compassion for people.
- It is to be committed to helping people not with a hand out, but with a hand up!
- We are to care for the homeless, the imprisoned, the hungry, the naked, the stranger, and the sick.
- Doing greater things occurs after we have mastered the art of living.

QUESTIONS FOR REFLECTION

- What can I do to show compassion to people that I am not currently doing now?
- What do I get passionate about in my life that can benefit others if I take action?
- What am I doing and who am I being in order to master the art of living?

CHAPTER 11

DO GREATER THINGS THROUGH GENEROSITY

Once we learn to grow in greater things spiritually, relationally, and financially, we will understand the significance of doing greater things through generosity. In fact, many of the stories in this book are about bigheartedness.

God wants us to be bighearted. God wants us to delight in doing greater things for others so that they can benefit and have greater things in their lives as well.

When this happens, everybody wins.

Did you know that every single day God gives us 86,400 seconds of life? One way to return that generosity is to bigheartedly give our time to others. We could, for example, mentor a child or an adult in our area of expertise, or volunteer at an inner-city sports league. We might also get together with a group of friends and offer to do yard work for an elderly person. The possibilities are endless.

One way to give our time meaningfully is to find a need and fill it. If you see a need in your community, you might just be the person to fill it.

Another way is to utilize your talents to help others. If you are a musician or vocalist, use your talent to brighten someone's life. If you are good with numbers, volunteer to help a nonprofit organization with bookkeeping. If you are sharp with technology, offer to help a nonprofit with its computers or Web site. There are as many possibilities as there are people with various talents and abilities. You are gifted for a purpose! Use that gift to add purpose in someone's life.

Another area in generosity is that of giving our possessions and finances to charitable causes. When we give, we find joy. The Grow in Greater Things section on finances laid the foundation for this type of generosity.

"'Bring the whole tithe into the storehouse, that there may be food in my house. Test me in this,' says the Lord Almighty, 'and see if I will not throw open the floodgates of heaven and pour out so much blessing that you will not have room enough for it'" (Malachi 3:10). Wow! What a promise! God wants us to bring a tithe to him so that we can experience the amazing results of faith.

Those words exhort us to change the way we think about our possessions. God wants us to see beyond the everyday to the every-way!

But this promise was born out of a problem. The people were withholding their tithes—ten percent of all they had—and society depended on people tithing to the temple storehouses. Social services to feed the hungry, to provide clothing for the poor, to help orphans and widows, and to care for the sick and ill were failing. Suffering was increasing. The social fabric was deteriorating. Crime was escalating. Greed was consuming all values. The social ministries of the temple were failing. The priests were even going hungry.

Society was in trouble. Why? God's people were withholding their tithes from Him. In fact, God even says that withholding generosity and tithes is an act of robbing from Him and, hence, the cause of all those troubles. But the wonderful nature of God's love is such that, instead of threatening the people, He acts entrepreneurially and says, "Test me in this." Look at the text again:

> Bring the whole tithe into the storehouse, that there may be food in my house. Test me in this, says the Lord Almighty, and see if I will not throw open the floodgates of heaven and pour out so much blessing that you will not have room enough for it. Malachi 3:10

That is amazing, isn't it? It reminds me of the statement that it is more blessed to give than it is to receive! "Test me in this and see if I will not throw open the floodgates of heaven and pour out so much blessing that you will not have room enough for it!" Wow!

I remember taking a class on perspectives of food and world hunger. For an entire semester we studied about the abundance of food produce worldwide and the level of starvation that still persisted despite that abundance. It was amazingly sad. And it all came down to how corporations, governments, individuals, and societies manage their resources. Much of it came down to politics and economics. If only we learn to see it and manage the abundance of wealth that we have properly we could eradicate hunger and poverty.

What would happen if those of us who Expect Greater Things and grow in greater things take the next step and do greater things with the spiritual wealth management of our time, talent, and material possessions? I believe that the world would change. Our nation would move from being one of the wealthiest to being one of the most significant. If we do greater things with our life's resources, we will see huge societal needs addressed and amazing things happen through our generosity!

The remaining chapters will offer tangible examples of wealth management and generosity. I will share several real-life examples of Greater Things champions who are making a difference in their communities because of their passion for living life to the fullest! It is my hope that these stories will inspire you to do greater things.

POINTS TO PONDER

- God wants us to be bighearted. When this happens, everybody wins.
- One way to give our time meaningfully is to find a need and fill it. If you see a need in your community, you might just be the person to fill it.
- God says, "Test Me in this."
- If we do greater things with our life's resources, we will see huge societal needs addressed and amazing things happen through our generosity!

QUESTIONS FOR REFLECTION

- What am I doing with my 86,400 seconds given to me everyday of my life?
- How am I using my time for the purpose of helping others?
- What special talents do I have that can enhance others' lives?
- Do I have the faith to take God at his word and test the teaching about giving?
- How can I get involved in helping to change the world through principles of generosity?

CHAPTER 12

DO GREATER THINGS FOR YOUR COMMUNITY: GREATER THINGS CHAMPIONS

Pat Owen
Fort Lauderdale, Florida

Second Chance Society

I am privileged to have some wonderful friends who live a Do Greater Things lifestyle and share their time, talents, and resources with the less fortunate. They make a difference. I hope you enjoy their stories and that they inspire you to do greater things in your own communities! They are truly Greater Things champions.

Everybody deserves a second chance!

When I first arrived at First United Methodist Church in Fort Lauderdale, Florida, in April 2000, there was much to learn and many great people to meet. As soon as I crossed the Georgia state line into Florida, I got "sand in my shoes." This is a Floridian's way of saying that I fell in the love with Florida and its diversity, both culturally and geographically. And, of course, the 3000 hours of sunshine, the average temperature of 77 degrees, the beaches, the golf courses, fishing, swimming, and year-round bicycling and shorts weather . . . well, you get the picture!

One of the first meetings was with a woman in my church. She scheduled an appointment and met with me in my office. She said, "Dr. John, my name is Pat. We are so glad to have you as our pastor. Now, let's get down to business. My husband, rest his soul, and I bought a building to house our business. Recently I consolidated all of my operations into another building. I sold the building that my husband and I purchased for a nice profit. However, I don't want to go out and spend the money. I want to use the money for something greater than myself. I want to set up a society that will give people a second chance. And I want your help in figuring out how we can do it." Wow! Talk about expecting, growing, and doing greater things to the glory of God.

I suggested several outstanding social service and ministry related agencies that worked with the homeless and the addicted. My thought was not to reinvent the wheel, but to look for a niche with unmet needs. I suggested that we could perhaps help people make the transition from the social and ministry programs to sustained self-sufficiency.

I asked her, "How much do you have to begin this work?" She answered, "$270,000." The Second Chance Society was born out of that meeting. Its purpose is to help those who have successfully gone through the local homeless ministries and county programs, or other rehab programs, so that they don't fall through the cracks and end up back where they started. In the past two years the Second Chance Society has helped hundreds of people. The vision is to create Second Chance Societies all over the nation.

Every two months we have a Second Chance Society dinner at our church in the fellowship hall. Community leaders, church members, social-sector leaders, and the benefactors of Second Chance's mission all gather around tables in the fellowship hall. We pray together, share a wonderful meal, and hear testimonies of how Second Chance is impacting lives. Here are a few examples:

One man needed tools so he could get a job. Second Chance bought him tools.

A woman needed to take a class to meet the necessary educational requirements for a secretarial position. Second Chance paid her tuition.

Another man needed to repair his truck so he could drive to the construction site. Second Chance paid for the repair work.

A man needed roofing boots so he could tar roofs in the hot Florida sun. Second Chance bought the man new boots.

The list goes on and on. Second Chance helps people when they are down, people who don't need a handout, but a hand up! The motto of the organization is: "Helping persons achieve self-sufficiency."

Pat is a wonderful example of one person who, because of her love for God and her neighbors, decided to do greater things with her life.

If we live with a Greater Things lifestyle, we will be amazed by the fresh thoughts that will grace our people, communities, businesses, faith communities, nation, and world. We will be amazed by the grassroots Do Greater Things activities that will identify and fulfill various needs!

If the faithful in our nation passionately helped their people to grow in greater things, the broad, deep, powerful, and life-changing grace of God would impact them as they exercised their faith. And we would, thereby, restore power to religion. The result will be thoughtful people who ask, "How can I do a greater thing with my life to make a difference in the world?"

Another great story about helping others occurs in Southern California.

Mark and Cherilyn Sheets-Moehlman

Newport Beach, California

Founders of the Children's Dental Center Inglewood, California

Cherilyn Sheets, DDS, and her husband, Mark Moelhman (aka Robin Hood) had a vision to provide free dental care to the children of Inglewood, California, in East Los Angeles—the backdrop for the movie *Grand Canyon*. The area is known for its high crime rate and poverty. In its heyday, Inglewood was a trendy community.

This is the community in which Cherilyn was raised. Her father, also a dentist, practiced in a building directly across the street from his lovely California ranch home. The palm tree lined street proclaimed a community of elegance and upward mobility. Dr. Sheets' patients included business, community, entertainment, and religious leaders noted for their commitment to excellence.

Time changed the Inglewood community. The palm trees now serve as reminders of the elegant days of past. The rusty cars, unkempt houses and yards, and chain-linked fences with razor wire around businesses speak of the stark reality today.

Cherilyn inherited the family home and dental office when her father passed away. She and Mark were faced with the challenge of what to do with the property. Through a series of circumstances, they decided to give back by doing a greater thing: creating the Children's Dental Center.

The Center is not a religious organization, although its founders have strong faith in God. Here is a description of their work and mission:

The Children's Dental Center opened its doors in Inglewood, California, in December 1995. Since then, the state-of-the-art facility has been staffed by dentists and hygienists—paid personnel, students, and volunteers—devoted to providing much-needed dental services and educational programs in an atmosphere of positive reinforcement for children without access to dental care.

> Our Mission
>
> The Children's Dental Center provides the highest quality multidisciplinary care to children who have no other access to dentistry and promotes their positive health behaviors. The dignity of the child is preserved in a comprehensive program emphasizing total health and prevention, while enhancing each child's positive self-image.
>
> The Children's Dental Center is an integral part of family and community life, and serves as an innovative, private-sector prototype for other centers throughout the country. The Center serves as a training ground for future generations of specialists in pediatric care and community service.

Based on this mission statement, an attractive, child-oriented space was created. A board of directors was developed and important partnerships were established to ensure the organization's sustained strength and success. These partnerships included local schools of dentistry, hospitals, school districts, the dental professional community, dental supply companies, and private and public foundations.

The Children's Dental Center represents an opportunity for people to be part of a truly significant project. It demonstrates what health care of the future could be: not a handout, but a "hand up" to those who want to help themselves. We invite your participation!

In addition to the Center, the Moehlmans also founded the Toothfairy Cottage. It is located in the home where Cherilyn was raised, across the street from the Children's Dental Center. The Toothfairy Cottage's goal is as follows:

> To expand and intensify the impact of The Children's Dental Center, we have created The Shannon Kelly Toothfairy Cottage—a learning center and administrative office—in a facility across the street from the Center. This new facility is named in memory of Shannon Kelly, a young woman who represents the Center's significant purpose and extraordinary spirit.

The Children's Dental Center provides educational messages in its operatories, at its education center, in school classrooms, and in after-school programs on three broad topics: oral hygiene; nutrition; and tobacco avoidance. The Toothfairy Cottage houses the oral health education programs. Emphasis is placed on youth, ages five through thirteen, where early intervention will have the greatest long-term impact (to learn more about the Center and the Toothfairy Cottage, please visit www.toothfairycottage.org).

National Children's Oral Health Foundation (NCOHF)—dental professionals, industry leaders, philanthropic individuals, and concerned nonprofit agencies.

Together, we're united in a mission that leaves no child behind.

Within the next 10 years, NCOHF network of affiliate centers will:

- Treat 5 million+ children most in need through more than 500 centers throughout the United States, and begin providing global support to developing nations.

- Educate and screen 20 million+ children through schools, community events, and ongoing community based prevention activities.

Our Mission:

To eliminate pediatric oral disease and promote overall health and well-being for millions of economically disadvantaged children, by serving as a comprehensive resource provider for not-for-profit pediatric oral health facilities, which deliver critical preventive, educational, and treatment services.

We seek partners who share our passion to improve the lives of children, now!

History

In 1995 Dr. Cherilyn Sheets led the establishment of The Children's Dental Center (TCDC) in Inglewood, California. Creating a dental home for disadvantaged children, TCDC provides immediate dental care for urgent oral health problems, restorative treatment services, preventative therapies, and a comprehensive child/parent preventive educational program. TCDC's compelling prototype model, which incorporates an innovative educational approach to oral health, has inspired the establishment of similar children's dental centers in other communities across the nation, including Philadelphia and Orange County in California.

While these efforts were exemplary, there remains an escalating need for quality dental care and preventive services as highlighted in numerous publications, including the Surgeon General's report: *Oral Health in America*. The National Children's Dental Foundation (TNCDF) was launched in February 2006 with the goal of linking hundreds of nonprofit pediatric community-based dental centers (Affiliates) treating 5 million children, and impacting millions more through educational programs.

The Foundation brought together dental and public health professionals, educators, corporate executives and employees, civic leaders, and concerned individuals to focus on the singular issue of delivery of quality pediatric oral health care.

Towards the end of its first year, the organization's name was changed to the National Children's Oral Health Foundation (NCOHF). The new name reflects the organization's integrated approach, connecting oral health with systemic health. NCOHF is engaging a broad range of stakeholders from dental, medical, and public health professionals, to universities, national organizations, corporate executives, civic leaders, and philanthropic parties in order to mount the powerful offensive campaign necessary to obliterate this "silent epidemic," and literally transform pain and suffering into healthy smiles and bright futures for millions of children.

With significant support from corporations, media partners, and dental professionals, NCOHF had approximately 50 nonprofit pediatric facilities in its Affiliate pipeline by the close of its first year of operations.

During this upcoming year, NCOHF will continue to expand its Affiliate network, launch the Virtual Learning Institute (VLI), and initiate community-based Toothfairy Projects to increase pediatric awareness of pediatric oral disease, while raising funds to support the delivery of critical oral health services.

Another story about a person of faith who is doing greater things occurs in New York, New York; South Bend, Indiana; and Phoenix, Arizona. One person's vision inspired leaders to rise up and is helping tens of thousands of inner-city children across the nation and around the world.

Bill Wilson
Brooklyn, New York

Sidewalk Sunday School

My friend and colleague Bill Wilson, from Brooklyn, New York, invited me to observe his Sidewalk Sunday School ministry up close. It was an invitation I couldn't pass up. So I packed my suitcase and left a very comfortable home in Granger, Indiana, to live for a week in a rat-infested warehouse in the heart of Brooklyn's ghetto.

I learned of Bill Wilson's work and mission through an organization called Churches Uniting in Global Mission (CUGM). Bill was our guest speaker at the Crystal Cathedral meeting of sixty clergy from various denominations. The group consisted of leading clergy from mainline, holiness, charismatic, Roman Catholic, and Greek Orthodox churches. The only prerequisites for membership were a proven record of significant leadership within his/her denomination and a strong commitment to Christology, to evangelism, and to the mission. The vision of CUGM is to accomplish together what we could not accomplish apart.

Bill spoke passionately about his vision for reaching children under the age of twelve before drugs, prostitution, street crime, and illiteracy did. He told his story. He was abandoned by his mother on an overpass in St. Petersburg, Florida, as a young boy. He related how a Christian man found him sitting on the overpass and took him home. Later the man took him to a Christian camp where Bill learned that God loved him, cared for him, and would never abandon him. Bill heard his calling and followed through by reaching out to children abandoned by their family, school, and society. He wanted them to know of God's immeasurable love for them!

He now ministers to over 20,000 children every week through Sidewalk Sunday School in the boroughs of New York City. In addition, the concept has spread throughout the globe. This Do Greater Things ministry is based on principles, not personalities.

To this day, Bill drives a bus when it is time to pick up the kids for Sidewalk Sunday School. He poignantly tells his supporters and audiences across the nation, "When I pick up one of those kids, I am picking myself up."

Bill's passion for doing greater things now extends around the globe! Hundreds of Sidewalk Sunday School ministries are springing up across America in communities of every kind. Scores of faith communities from every denomination are utilizing the principles of Sidewalk Sunday School to reach the inner-city children. Lives are being changed! This is a Greater Things success story.

Here is a description of the work from the Metro Ministries Web site:

Since 1980 Bill Wilson and Metro Ministries have pioneered the human wasteland of America's forgotten inner cities. Their mission is to find and rescue the children left behind in this battleground of drugs, violence, abuse, and filth. After throwing out the old rule books, Bill developed an effective Sunday school ministry that had to work in the chaos and violence of the inner city. This was a struggle that could only be won with the power of God. With enormous faith and persistence, Bill began Sunday schools and the Won-By-One Children's Sponsorship Program, a unique way to partner Christians across America with an inner-city child.

Along the way, Bill Wilson built a professional staff totally dedicated to changing America one child at a time. Each week, just by traveling within two miles of the ministry center in Brooklyn, their buses and buildings began filling with children who looked to Metro Ministries Sunday School as the best and brightest time of their lives.

This Do Greater Things work has had a ripple effect across the globe, my former congregation in South Bend, Indiana, being part of that ripple. It was there, in 1995, that I invited Bill Wilson to share his vision for Sidewalk Sunday School.

Bill's effective preaching and teaching netted the following:
1. A Sidewalk Sunday School truck for the Bronx sponsored by the Clay United Methodist Church.
2. A Sidewalk Sunday School ministry launched to reach the inner-city children of South Bend, Indiana. Over 120 volunteers from the church ministered to over 350 children each week. The ministry still continues to be effective!
3. A church member became a full-time director of Sidewalk Sunday School for the United Methodist Church in the Desert Southwest Conference. Billie Fidlin is helping people Do Greater Things in reaching children throughout the United States!

Here is an excerpt from the Desert Southwest Conference's Sidewalk Sunday School Web site that describes this important work:

> Welcome to the Sidewalk Sunday School web page for the Desert Southwest Annual Conference. I am happy that you have decided to learn more about the exciting methodology of street evangelism, originated by Reverend Bill Wilson of Metro Ministries.
>
> The Sidewalk Sunday School Ministry focuses on teaching urban children and their families the fundamentals of Christianity: teaching empowerment through Christ to turn away from the negative community cycles that face them, and to turn their hearts, minds, and actions toward a lifestyle that contains promise and hope for the future.
>
> The Sidewalk Sunday School Ministry in its ideal model uses a box truck (i.e., a 14-feet U-Haul, Pensky, Ryder, etc.), converted into a portable platform church. The truck contains its own sound system, cupboards and counters for storage and work space, and everything necessary for a resounding worship service on the streets. Our volunteers travel to the same site(s) each week, spreading the Good News of the Risen Lord. Our mission is to help the unchurched children, youth, gang members, homeless people, family members,

and anyone else hear that there is someone who loves them, who wants and desires a personal relationship with them, who considers them God's most precious child. Our street worship is for those who have yet to hear, those who have already heard, and for those who need to hear again, the name and love of Jesus Christ.

This high-energy weekly ministry includes music, drama, Bible object lessons and stories, games, prizes, prayers, promotions, and more! Each exciting minute is packed with innovative ministry approaches for communicating the one central weekly biblical theme.

But Sidewalk doesn't stop at the worship service! All children and families are visited each week by their own personal visitation team. This is where the real relationships of Sidewalk are built. This is also where we learn of extended ministry opportunities. What is the need particular to the site? (Note: needs differ site to site, even within the same city.) Churches may elect to meet the needs learned through the visitation routes; for example, the need for food might be identified, so the church begins a food-pantry ministry. Many times our churches have responded to the community needs, and have also become "experts" in networking—knowing what services already exist, and how to put our families in touch with those services.

Also critical to our ministry is prayer. We take prayer requests from our faith community each week, and the site's prayer team prays daily over those requests. We have literally hundreds of people involved on our site prayer teams. These teams also include people who are homebound and disabled so that they too may be involved in their own vital ministry again. We also have an international prayer team, which includes Sidewalk prayer warriors from across the United States, Africa, Japan, Hungary, and France. The international team is reserved for requests regarding serious illness, death, and Sidewalk expansion, or site requests. We, together, are in community. This is the dream. I pray that you will help make the dream a reality.

This is truly a Do Greater Things effort!

A VISIT TO BILL WILSON'S NEW YORK

Once I heard the above story in the mid-90s, I had to see its operations first hand. So I packed my bag and headed for New York City. Bill picked me up at the airport. We drove past Yankee Stadium and the site of the 1966 World's Fair. Soon the Manhattan skyline came into view and then receded in the rearview mirror as we crossed the bridge into Brooklyn. As we drove deeper into the borough and the ghetto, I was amazed to see bullet holes in the sides of buildings and cars. Gang graffiti adorned the storefronts. Much of the graffiti was colorful, but had a dark message: RIP. Bill told me these messages were painted at specific places where gang members had been shot or stabbed to death. The graffiti was prevalent throughout the area. It was chilling.

The trip was busy and enjoyable! It was exciting to see children throughout the projects come to Sidewalk Sunday School. Their energy was contagious. It was undeniably the best part of the children's week. When I asked Bill why it was so important to reach the children before they turned twelve, his reply was quick and decisive: "We have to get them before drugs, alcohol, gangs, or prostitution do. If we don't get them before the age of twelve, we won't get them!"

Bill's insight is supported by a recent study of the Barna Research Group that points out the importance of placing resources into reaching and shaping the spiritual lives of children between four to thirteen years of age.

George Barna of the Barna Research Group states that people-of-faith communities must focus on shaping the faith and morals of America's children. He says that it is the single most important work that we need to do!

Each child, whether living in a ghetto or in middle- or upper-class America, needs solid spiritual and moral teaching that will help shape his or her character. If people of faith, through their generosity, don't build programs to cater to that need, who will? This is definitely a Do Greater Things opportunity for each one of us to take seriously.

A DINNER PARTY WITH THE HOMELESS

One Thursday evening, during my visit to the Brooklyn ghetto with Bill, I was invited to a dinner party. This wasn't just any dinner party. It was held under the Brooklyn Bridge by the East River on the Brooklyn side. Bill said, "Doc, join me for dinner with the homeless guys and gals by the river. I take them KFC each week. We talk, shoot the breeze, and have dinner together. I pray for them and they pray for me. It's just a little something I like to do each week."

So I accepted the dinner invitation. Bill and I drove to KFC and picked up about $100 worth of food. Then we made our way to the homeless village by the East River. A contractor had created several huts with enough space for sleeping; the huts had no doors. Only a blanket or sheet created a veil that pretended to keep out intruders. Many of the homeless placed their prized possessions on top of the huts. The roof was made of corrugated plastic strong enough to support each inhabitant's belongings. An unspoken code of ethics implied the roof tops to be off-limits.

Several of the homeless gathered in a circle when Bill and I brought dinner. They pulled up rat-chewed easy chairs, upside-down plastic pickle buckets, and other makeshift chairs. We passed the food around, and Bill asked how they were doing. One man, John, stood out in particular.

John was a plumber by trade who had a falling out with his parents and wife. He did not want to work. He chose to live in homelessness because he didn't want to repair the broken relationships. John had a terrible wound on his arm, and to treat it, he had stolen a suture kit from a nearby hospital and sewn the wound himself.

Several large river rats scampered near the dinner party at the smell of the KFC. As John was telling his story, one rat actually came within two feet of us and scampered off with a discarded chicken bone. I noticed the homeless people watch, flinch, and huddle closer to themselves with the food. I asked John if this was a regular occurrence. He answered "Yes." Then I said, "When do you adjust to having rats live so near by you?" He answered by telling me a story about his first night there.

Someone had found leftover spaghetti at an Italian restaurant. They brought it and shared it with John, who ate until he was full. Then he decided to take the plate of leftover spaghetti into his hut. He placed the plate next to his bed while he slept. When he woke up, the entire plate had been licked clean by the rats. "Sir, I have lived here for ninety-five days. Maybe I will get used to it on day ninety-six," he said.

John told us his prayer concerns, thanked us for the food, and asked us to pray with him. He talked about his life in the United States Army while in Viet Nam. As we finished our time with John and the other homeless people, I asked Bill if any of them would get out of the homeless life. He said, "It is tough. In the meantime, we can bring food, faith, and hope."

Since that dinner with the homeless, our friend John passed away. He died a homeless man in one of the wealthiest cities and nations in the world. This underscores the importance of each of us doing greater things with our lives and resources; the action will strengthen the social fabric so that it becomes a safety net for the down-and-outs, one from which they can pull themselves up with a hand up, not a handout.

These stories regarding the homeless and the Sidewalk Sunday School are examples of how expecting greater things and growing in greater things can lead us to Do Greater Things!

Raymond Bechard and Ahava Kids

Old Saybrook, Connecticut

Since 1990 Raymond Bechard has traveled the globe to save the world's most valuable and vulnerable citizens: children. From the United States to Israel, Russia, Europe, Haiti, Latin America, and beyond, Ray has built a network of dedicated people who devote their lives to protecting children from evil and providing them with a better, safer life.

Today, he is the founder and president of Ahava Kids, a human-rights organization based in the United States. Ahava Kids exists for one reason: to rescue orphaned young people from the crime of child trafficking, enslavement, and exploitation throughout the world. The organization's objective is to support and actively work with others around the world that put themselves between children and whatever malevolence they may face. They protect and defend these children in order to lift them up to a better life. This is truly a Do Greater Things effort.

Ray has developed the process of *Raid, Rescue, Relocation,* and *Rehabilitation* to save as many young people as possible. This four-step procedure is most effective in removing young people from the dangers of trafficking and giving them the best chance at a decent life. Ahava Kids is different because they directly provide resources to the people risking their lives every day for these children. These are local people who know the culture and the social and legal systems. They work in places most of us can't go or just don't want to go.

Ray's book, *Unspeakable: The Hidden Truth Behind the World's Fastest Growing Crime,* is an expose of international child trafficking and organized crime's involvement in it. Raymond tells us, "Exposing this global attack against children is one of the most important missions of Ahava Kids. Most people don't want to look at the places where this crime takes place. They do not want to experience what it is like to walk through the back alleys, the brothels, the battlefields, and even the magnificent mansions where children are bought and sold into modern day slavery. Most people do not want to go where I go. But, to save children from the most horrible abuse imaginable, we must all find the courage to reach into the darkness and save the children hiding there. Together, we must speak for the children who are trapped in a life of silent torture."

The inspiration for Ahava Kids came after Raymond's experiences working with a support group near Ground Zero in New York City after the 9/11 attacks. They were very close to the massive pile of rubble. He describes it this way, "You couldn't walk more than a block without someone approaching you with photos in their hands. They would look at you with pleading eyes, eyes that would stop you in your tracks. They would each hand you a copy of the photo they were carrying and say something like, 'This is a picture of my brother.' Or, 'This is my friend, Rob.' And you would look at the picture carefully while they told you that the person in the photo was missing. 'Have you seen anyone who looks like this?' 'If you see them, can you call this number?'"

Bechard says that those near the remains of the World Trade Center could see that anyone escaping the disaster would be a miracle. Walking near it was dangerous. There would be no more survivors. "But that didn't matter," he says, "because this person with the photographs was desperate for hope. You have to be very careful with people in that frame of mind. I couldn't look at them—into those pleading eyes—and tell them the truth; that the person they treasured is gone forever. So I would take each photo that was given to me on the streets and look at every one of them carefully and say respectfully, 'Yes, I'll look around.' Yes, if I see your loved one, I will call you right away.'"

Ray told me that he hated seeing the desperate and helpless look in their eyes and feeling so powerless. No matter how hard he tried, there was nothing he could do; nothing he tried would ever make a difference.

Several months later, he was in Haiti, working at a small orphanage. Several children there had HIV/AIDS. Many had been bought and sold on the child-trafficking market for a variety of reasons, but all of them were lucky to have been rescued and brought to this simple sanctuary. By then, Bechard had already heard a great deal about child trafficking, having consulted with several organizations fighting injustice in many ways, but he had never been this close to the victims. He said, "One little girl sat on my lap while the nurse administered her medication. It consisted of an 'AIDS Cocktail' of drugs that was mixed in a syrup which made it easier for her to swallow. The mixture was placed in a tube that pushed the drugs down into her throat very quickly. She shuddered a little bit once the medication made its way into her stomach. Then she looked up at me with *those* eyes, the same pleading eyes I had seen on the dusty streets of New York. Eyes looking for an answer . . . eyes looking for hope. This time I wasn't going to hedge the truth. This time, I knew I could do something about it. I could make a difference."

He told the little girl everything was going to be okay; that she was safe. Since then Ray has dedicated himself to keeping that promise.

Ray travels all over the world to find the best ways to fight child trafficking while getting to know the people who are doing whatever it takes to intervene and save the children. He discovered that trafficking exists in every community in the world. "But I also found the hope for which I was looking," he explains. "Because wherever trafficking occurs, there are good and courageous people willing to fight for the victims no matter how dangerous the people are who run the trafficking schemes."

Ray believes it is our job to show these millions of children that they deserve to be loved. That is why Ahava Kids (Ahava is a Hebrew word which literally means love) go to extremes for each child. They go overboard in showing the children how much they are valued. They play with them for hours, until they fall asleep from exhaustion. They give them little parties for no reason. They try to discover what, if any, their dreams are, and then they try to make them come true. They do whatever it takes to prove to the children that they are worth loving unconditionally, and that they are worth *everything and more.*

Of course, all of this takes enormous amounts of work, time, and money. Most of all it takes dedicated people who understand that sacrifices must be made for these children. Bechard summarizes his work this way, "It is amazing to see the changes in children when they realize someone has made a sacrifice for them. Something in their mind is transformed. It is hard for them to believe that someone, anyone, would give up something in order to make them feel better. Yet people willing to do this kind of work are rare."

Raymond Bechard is a Greater Things champion who has learned to convert faith into action!

David and Jean Eastman-Carruthers

Fort Lauderdale, Florida

Buktoof and Friends

My good friends, David Carruthers and his wife Jean Eastman Carruthers, are extremely creative business people who love to do greater things with their lives. David is a land and real estate developer, and Jean is an artist and clothing designer. Several years ago they created a cartoon character named Buktoof, as well as several other cartoon friends. Buktoof and friends are committed to telling stories about friendship, diversity, ethics, values, beliefs, the environment, and other critically important lessons. Recently, a large company with offices in Atlanta and Fort Lauderdale licensed Bucktoof for a green campaign! Reportedly, the company's employees have enjoyed the campaign so much that they are actively participating and saving energy.

> David tells the story best:
>
> [The] "Buktoof & Friends" idea came about as something that could help children and parents. We both believe that every one of us is put on this earth for a special purpose . . . to Do Greater Things. People always search, and we are no different. Jean and I were both raised to be kind and to help in any way that would express goodwill to others. We both started to think, as we saw an increase in violence, bad manners, disrespect, lack of physical activity, and a decline in public educational standards, that we could do something with our skill set to make a positive difference. Something needs to counteract the negative content

Do Greater Things for Your Community: Greater Things Champions

available through the Internet, video games, and TV. We decided that there had to be a better way to express good family values.

At Buktoof the mission is to instill a return to core values. We are offering non-violent programming, a return to kindness and the days of 'Please and Thank You.' Through Buktoof & Friends, Jean and I wanted to bring the connection back to the family unit, by involvement of parents with their children in schooling, exercise, and overall health. At the same time we both wanted to make the lives of our members easier by putting what they need and use everyday on one site: kind of a one-stop site. Things like shopping, school links, travel, financial aid, local events, and weather, as well as answering health questions to mention a few things. Most importantly, Buktoof and Friends members will have fun with games, chat rooms, contests, fun exercises, and good, clean family entertainment.

Children are constantly approached on the Internet by all types of questionable individuals. The Buktoof security services that will be offered to its members on the net will enable families to feel more comfortable about allowing their children to enjoy safely interacting with other members of Buktoof. As for TV and video games, Buktoof and Friends cartoons will also have funny and educational programs for all types of families.

Buktoof is thrilled to be associated with Children's Health Foundation, a nonprofit charity organization dedicated to helping children. This charity is recognized by and teamed up with major hospitals and doctors to provide surgeries and procedures to less fortunate children.

Wayne and Lynda Evans

Jupiter, Florida

Kids Depot Realty and Tithing

The Evans are great friends of mine who have a deep passion for God's love, a strong sense of purpose, and a heart for bringing out greater things in their every involvement, be it their business, investments, personal friendships, gifts to higher education, or tithes to their church.

Wayne is a towering man of six feet, eight inches. Lynda is a small, beautiful woman who is five feet, two inches tall! They command a presence whenever they enter a room together. They exude a passion for life and a love for God. Wayne has a plaque on his desk that reads: "May all who come behind us find us faithful."

Wayne and Lynda founded a company called Kid's Depot Realty several years ago. In short, they buy and sell day care centers throughout South Florida. Their business model is excellent because it is based on principle, not profit, and, in exercising this business ethic, they have also proven to be highly successful in managing their company. The basic principles by which they operate their company are these: do potential buyers want to make a difference in children's lives by teaching them ethics, trust, faith, spirituality, and hope, or do the buyers just want to turn a profit? If the answer is the latter, then Kid's Depot Realty won't enter into business with them. Why? It's about the children and not about the money. This principle and purpose provides Wayne and Lynda with a great amount of business with people with whom they enjoy doing business.

- The second principle guides them to focus on hiring people who share their same spiritual value system. This is true at their corporate offices that overlook the Intercoastal Waterway and beautiful Jupiter Island. It is also true at each of their day care centers. In fact, if a director or a teacher of a facility they are purchasing doesn't embody solid ethics and values, Wayne and Linda will give the person an opportunity to get in line with their corporate ethic. In this case, the corporate ethic is being committed to family and children while living a life that is pleasing to God. This scenario reflects an ever-increasing desire for spirituality in corporate America where profit is achieved through a balance of work ethic and life ethic, while enjoying a meaningful life.

- Another ethic that guides their business is the desire to make a difference one child and one community at a time. Two of their facilities are located in a very poor part of South Florida. The number of unwed mothers is quite high, and a disabling sense of poverty pervades the community. There is a sense that people are in a hole they will never get out of! Values, ethics, and spirituality are often neglected for immediate gratification and the fast buck. Wayne and Lynda utilize their influence as business owners and leaders to set a new standard that underscores values, ethics, and spirituality, one that calls people to expect greater things for their lives. And, through accredited industry standards, they equip their employees and the children they serve with a corporate value system that calls for a higher plane of living. This process results in one teacher at a time finding hope who, in turn, gives hope to the children he or she serves. Those children take the hope to their homes. The result, over time, is like water dripping on a rock. The rock changes. This same principle can be employed in areas experiencing economic, spiritual, ethical, and moral depression. Hope can change things, people, and communities. Wayne and Lynda are examples of people who live by the courage of their convictions and apply them to their business.

The Evans consistently use the same spiritual ethic that guides their business in their investments and other business relationships. I saw this first hand when I brought an investment opportunity to them. It involved diamonds! I recently met a man who had been involved in the diamond business in West Africa. I met him at a wedding that I performed in Naples, Florida, at the Ritz Carlton on the Gulf of Mexico. We sat next to each other at the reception. He told me how he had been involved in the blood diamond trade in West Africa. I asked him if the movie *Blood Diamond* had any truth to it. He said that the level of death and destruction that had occurred during those years had been toned down.

He told me that the horror of the experience had led him to a dramatic conversion, after which he developed a business plan that would incorporate the Kimberly Process to transform rough diamonds in the mines into cut diamonds to be sold at retail stores; the plan would guarantee no involvement of blood diamonds. I was impressed with this, but the next thing that he said truly sold me on the plan. He said that the people of West Africa in the French Province of Guinea where the mines are located have no infrastructure of roads, hospitals, schools, worship centers, running water, sewage, electricity, or safe housing. His goal was to utilize, as a way of giving back to the community, some of his profits to raise the miners' standard of living. Whereas the rebels who ran the trade in blood diamonds raped and pillaged, this plan, which embraces the Kimberly Process, will give back substantially to the people.

Wayne and Lynda, after several meetings with me and the founder of the company, determined that his spiritual ethic not only fit theirs, but that it would also produce a substantial profit for everyone involved. Wayne said, "I like this! It helps others and provides a large profit. We will take whatever profit is gained and tithe at least ten percent of it to our church. That will provide the resources necessary to turn the church around and help a lot of people know God's love! We believe that to be good stewards anointed by God, we must tithe and gift at least twenty percent to directly support Christ-centered projects." In fact, I know that the Evans live this Do Greater Things ethic through their support of the First United Methodist Church of Jupiter/Tequesta, Florida; of Gideons International; of Wayland Baptist University in Planeview, Texas (Wayne's alma matter where he played basketball); and of the

Golden Canes for Miami University Athletic programs. They are also supportive of Greater Things Enterprises.

The Evans exemplify real people who want to make a Greater Things difference. They understand that God gives us the ability to generate wealth to help others. They embrace John Wesley's teaching that says, "Gain all you can. Save all you can. Give all you can." They influence their family; the people who work with them; the businesses that they manage, buy, and sell; the investments they make; their church and college; and even the villagers in Guinea. This is truly a Do Greater Things attitude where faith meets life.

Wayne and Lynda said, "God has blessed us in so many ways and keeps putting opportunities in front of us. Sometimes the water holes are far apart. They're deep, but they're far apart." What a testimony to expecting greater things, growing in greater things, and doing greater things!

Wayne Huizenga

Businessman, Entrepreneur, and Philanthropist for Education

The first time I met Wayne and Marti Huizenga was at an event for charity on top of the Northern Trust Bank Building's rooftop garden in downtown Fort Lauderdale. I was in the beginning phases of my work as the pastor for the First United Methodist Church in the downtown area and was invited to the event.

Wayne and Marti were gracious to me in welcoming me to town and to South Florida. We chit-chatted and made small talk. Afterwards, we had very little contact for a few years. Of course, I read about Mr. Huizenga's many business dealings and the several philanthropic gifts that he and Marti bestowed on the community, especially Pine Crest Prep School. I watched with admiration as Nova Southeastern University's H. Wayne Huizenga School of Business and Entrepreneurship grew and influenced new business leaders in the areas of ethics, values, and integrity (which it still does).

If you google H. Wayne Huizenga you will discover that his is a true rags to riches story. Of course, you will find some curmudgeonly articles by those who are jealous of success and significance. You will also discover some wonderfully written accounts about his life and work. They depict a man of vision, integrity, tough business acumen, and proven results. Wayne's passion for life, family, faith, and the greater community at large will be his legacy. He and his wife, Marti, are definitely Greater Things Champions.

I began to know the Huizenga's more personally through my friendship that I established with Wayne's nephew, Steve Hudson, and the Hudson family. This friendship developed when I served as the pastor who performed Steve and Jeannie's wedding.

I have been involved in hundreds of premarital counselings and weddings in my many years of ministry. Steve, Jeannie, and I hit it off the first time that we met. In fact, each premarital counseling session lasted for two-and-a-half hours; they usually last for one. We had such a huge connection in terms of greater things thinking, that the minutes passed as seconds.

In short, we became great friends; so much so, that I was honored to officiate at Steve and Jeannie's wedding and other family events, including baptisms and the blessing of their new home in Fort Lauderdale.

Steve and Jeannie's wedding was amazing! The rehearsal was equally great. I'll never forget taking a cruise on the *Bon Bon* yacht. A 145 footer, on the intercoastal waterway in Broward County. The atmosphere was regal. The food was amazing. The refreshments outstanding. The passengers quite interesting!

I enjoyed much of the cruise on the aft deck. This was the first opportunity I had to get to know the Huizengas and Hudsons better. We talked about the Dolphins, the Marlins, Blockbuster, Waste Management, Autonation, traveling, golf, fishing, boating, family, and friends. I shared my vision of Greater Things. I told them how much I believed in seeing people empowered by expecting, growing in, and doing greater things.

Time passed and I was honored to celebrate the baptisms of Steve and Jeannie's babies, as well as the children of Holly and Scott, Steve's sister and brother-in-law.

I remember the brunch after the baby's baptism. It was a festive occasion held at Steve and Jeannie's home. Family and friends gathered to celebrate the sacrament of baptism and the gift of faith and family. Wayne had just been named "entrepreneur of the world." I congratulated him on this amazing honor. Then I asked Wayne and Marti what it was they were most proud of in their lives. Their answer delighted me. It wasn't their vast wealth. It wasn't their lovely homes. It wasn't all the bells and whistles that come with great financial success. It was their passion for higher education. It was their commitment to funding scholarships. Wayne and Marti told me that they fund 100 students each year. Each student receives a four-year college scholarship.

Their eyes filled with delight as they shared their story of how they award the scholarships. Each year, their friend and fellow Horatio Alger Society member Supreme Court Justice Clarence Thomas comes to Florida to help preside over the festivities. Their message is one of hope and inspiration.

Wayne and Justice Thomas both have rags to riches stories. They, along with many other notable Americans, including Dr. Robert H. Schuller, belong to the Horatio Alger Society. This is an invitation only society. Horatio Alger celebrates great Americans who lived the American Dream. They started with humble means, pulled themselves up by their own bootstraps, and made an impact in their chosen field. Then they gave back to their community, nation, and world. The Horatio Alger Society is filled with Greater Things Champions.

Wayne and Justice Thomas share their stories of struggle, success, and significance with the 100 scholarship recipients and their families. They call them to Expect Greater Things. They challenge them to be both successful and significant, personally and professionally.

To date, Wayne and Marti Huizenga have awarded over 500 scholarships. Think of the amazing ripple effect that Wayne and Marti are creating around the world due their vision and generosity.

Wayne and Marti understand the power of expecting greater things, growing in greater things, and doing greater things. They are truly Greater Things champions.

What can you do to create a Do Greater Things ripple effect? By utilizing an Expect Greater Things, Grow in Greater Things, and Do Greater Things lifestyle, you can make a huge difference in the lives of those around you and around the world!

THE POWER OF THE RIPPLE EFFECT

Think about it! What would happen if millions of people active in the 450,000 Protestant, Roman Catholic, Greek Orthodox, and

Eastern Orthodox churches were passionate about Doing Greater Things? These people represent thirty-three percent of the American population. What would happen if the sixty-two percent of the population who believe in God and seek spiritual growth but who don't worship in a church or synagogue decided to expect, grow, and do greater things with their lives?

Can you imagine the impact that God's people would have on our nation and the world? Can you imagine the impact the faith communities could have on their communities? Can you imagine the positive experience you would have because you are inspired to help the disenfranchised in our culture? Can you imagine the positive word that would spread about people of faith?

By implementing the Expect, Grow, and Do Greater Things philosophy you can turn around your life, your faith community, and your town. If enough of us join together, we could actually do a greater thing in our nation and the world. The possibilities are enormous! They are fantastic.

Dream with me, would you? Let's dream about what would happen in the world if every Christian tithed, if every Christian church tithed!

The churches across America have huge potential in terms of their giving power. There are 350,000 Protestant churches that produce a total revenue of $65 billion a year. It sounds like a lot of money, doesn't it? Four billion dollars is given to the United Methodist Church, while six billion is given to the Southern Baptist Church. On average, a Protestant gives 2.5 percent of his or her annual income to the church.

If the thirty-three percent of Americans who attend Protestant churches tithed, we would generate $260 billion per year. The Great Commission would be advanced. Our nation's children, 64 percent of whom don't go to church, would grow up knowing the spiritual truths of God's love. How would that happen? We'd have primetime television broadcasting shows on spiritual truths, ethics, and values. We'd have commercials about the family and God's love. We'd reach the children through the Internet, radio, television, and feature films. The outreach would be classy and have integrity; it would be spiritually meaningful, and it would draw them in and put them in a healthy local church where they could learn and be nurtured, loved, and cared for.

All that would happen if the church tithed. Then our nation's youth would grow up knowing the spiritual presence of God in the midst of tough teenage choices. Peer groups would be available for meet-and-greet sessions, as would materials that would help them understand the tough choices. And these materials would be on easy-to-access Web sites, podcasts, video phones, and the like. They would teach the youth that God values them and has a purpose for their lives that truly is empowering and exciting.

If the church tithed, our nation's adults could find hope during difficult times in their marriages. Those who have suffered divorce could find the peace of God through healthy relationship ministries that help deal with the root causes of their divorce so that the same mistakes don't happen again. The singles in our society, 50 percent of the population, would thrive because the church would have the necessary funding to develop ministries of meaning and purpose.

If the church tithed, we would move from being one of the world's richest countries to being the most significant. We'd have the financial backing to fulfill both the Great Commission and missions of justice and mercy. We would see the hungry fed, the naked clothed, and the sick healed. There would be few imprisoned, the homeless would have shelter and programs for self-sufficiency, and the spiritually dead would come alive through the power of God's love.

If the church tithed, we would need more schools, universities, and seminaries instead of prisons and jails. We'd need more office complexes because of booming businesses run on godly principles. We'd need more recreational and retreat facilities so people could advance their spiritual lives, if the church tithed.

In short, we would see the promise in Malachi fulfilled:

"'Bring the whole tithe into the storehouse, that there may be food in my house. Test me in this,' says the Lord Almighty, 'and see if I will not throw open the floodgates of heaven and pour out so much blessing that you will not have room enough for it (3:10).'"

We are blessed! Have an attitude of gratitude! Serve God fully. Let's achieve greater things.

And all of that is if *only* the Christians in the churches tithed! What would happen if every Expect Greater Things person of faith who doesn't attend a place of worship gave ten percent or more of his or her God-given wealth to various charities in gratitude to His generosity? That means 62 percent of Americans would be giving more generously than they currently do. The results would be amazing!

Perhaps world hunger could be eradicated through the empowerment of lobbyist in the halls of power and the boardrooms around the world. Infrastructures could be developed in Third World countries that could serve to advance education, business, tourism, and a host of social and political reforms. Perhaps lessons in the power of spiritually guided business, political, and social ethics and values could be imparted to people.

But that is a tall order. Every journey begins with the first step. What would be your first step? Perhaps it would be to decide today to become a Greater Things champion. Perhaps it would be to identify a need in your community that is not being addressed and to develop a plan to meet that need. The old business maxim is true, "Fail to plan, plan to fail." But it is also true that if you work the plan, the plan can work! Like everything else in life worth doing, it takes time and discipline to do greater things.

Doing greater things is giving when you feel like keeping, praying for others when you need to be prayed for, feeding others when your own soul is hungry, and living truth before people even when you can't see the results. Doing greater things is hurting with other people even when your own hurt can't be articulated. It is keeping your word even when it is not convenient; it is being faithful when you want to run away.

Doing greater things is a supranatural result of expecting and growing in greater things! We find our energy growing as we do greater things. Even when we grow weary we find energy that sustains and motivates us to move forward. In the process, we receive new inspiration and find new ways to accomplish greater things.

I invite you to think and pray about where you can use your talent, resources, skills, training, network of friends and associates, and passion to do greater things. Ask God to help you find the courage to act in faith and make a difference.

As you do so, you will enjoy the following benefits!

- Benefit #1: Your faith will be reinforced!
- Benefit #2: Your faith will make a tangible difference in another's life.
- Benefit #3: You will do greater things and bring glory to God!

So today, choose to be a Greater Things person!

Action 1: Expect Greater Things.
Action 2: Grow in Greater Things.
Action 3: Today, Decide to Do Greater Things!

I AM LOOKING FOR GREATER THINGS CHAMPIONS!

Do you know any Greater Things champions? I want to know their story! I want to celebrate their passion and perhaps include them and their work on our Web site (www.expectgreaterthings.com) and future publications. Please write to me and tell me their story. Or, if it is your story, I want to hear it! You can be a source of inspiration to tens of thousands of people to do greater things. So write me your stories or send me a video or materials so that we can work together to Do Greater Things!

POINTS TO PONDER

- Everybody deserves a second chance!
- If we live with a Greater Things lifestyle, we will be amazed by the fresh thoughts that will grace our people, communities, businesses, faith communities, nation, and world.
- By utilizing an Expect Greater Things, Grow in Greater Things, and Do Greater Things lifestyle, you I can make a huge difference in the lives of those around me and around the world!

QUESTIONS FOR REFLECTION

- What can I do to create a Do Greater Things ripple effect?
- What can I do to make this possibility a reality?

CHAPTER 13

DO GREATER THINGS ENVIRONMENTALLY

In the late 1990s I remember sitting in my office in South Bend, Indiana, on a beautiful, cold, and snowy winter's day. My office had a bank of windows twenty feet wide. It looked across the parking lot to the hilly, wooded neighborhood across a frozen pond. The intercom beeped. My administrative assistant said, "Dr. Myers, The Reverend David Scoates from the Crystal Cathedral in Garden Grove, California, and Churches United in Global Missions is on the line. Are you available?" Was I available? Absolutely! David was a dear friend, a treasured colleague, and a dynamic speaker and leader. We had been friends for several years and had traveled to Russia and throughout the United States on projects for Churches United in Global Missions. His wife, Vonda Kay Van Dyke Scoates, also a great friend and Miss America 1965, had been on many of those trips. We had been in each other's homes and actually planned to write a book together. So would I take the call? Absolutely. One of my favorite people in the world was on the line.

"John, the executive committee for CUGM met and would like to ask you to be the point person for the environment. It is going to be an ever increasingly important issue and we want you to spearhead it for us." I was caught off guard. After all, the environment is such a huge topic! Where do you start?

I remembered Mikhail Gorbachev's comments about the global environment and its link to spirituality during our April 24, 1992, meeting at the Gorbachev Foundation in Moscow, Russia. This is what he said:

> We are not just moving from one phase to another phase of development; we are really moving from one era, one epoch to another epoch. First of all, today the world, the whole world is integrated, interrelated, interlinked in every way. The problem of water resources, the problem of the atmosphere, that is our common problem. I think we either survive together or we die together; this is a tough formula . . . I think this is something that religious leaders should think about. We have to find a way to stimulate the spiritual element, the spiritual principle in man . . . We have to find a way to emphasize the spiritual.

Did you catch that? The former leader of the former Union of Soviet Socialist Republics, an atheistic state, knew the importance of speaking to the spiritual needs of people, as well as leading on environmental issues like the atmosphere and water resources. Mikhail Gorbachev said, "I understand that you are a serious group of spiritual leaders." Then he went on to ask us to lead and influence people so that the serious issues of our time could be addressed with integrity and strength.

The meeting with Mikhail Gorbachev helped underscore spiritual perspective in the global nature of Doing Greater Things Environmentally. We are spiritually responsible when we care for our environment.

"In the beginning God created . . ." (Genesis 1:1). That statement alone helps us to see the connection between the earth, the environment, and our relationship with God.

One of my favorite teachings from my student days at Duke was that God created everything that there is *ex nihilo*, which is a Latin term that means "out of nothing." In other words, God created everything out of nothing.

Some scientists attribute all creation to the big bang theory, which basically says that a power pellet the size of a golf ball exploded in the darkness and began the creation process. That's possible. But who created the ball? God created it out of nothing.

Evolutionists suggest that the world and humanity evolved over millions of years. But I still ask the question: who created the process? God created it out of nothing.

Some theologians say that the process of creation took six days, with the seventh day designated as a day of rest. Other theologians say that the Bible teaches that "a day is as a thousand years to the Lord and a thousand years is as a day." They would postulate that God created everything over a longer period than six days, perhaps millions of years.

For people of faith who expect greater things, grow in greater things, and do greater things, these positions are relatively meaningless. What does have meaning is that God created everything, including us, "out of nothing," and He expects us to do something great with our lives!

Part of that something great is to be a fantastic steward over God's creation that He entrusted to us. In fact, the Bible teaches us that God has given us authority over creation.

The bottom line is that God created everything and directed us to watch over and manage the creation and the environment. The Psalmist writes,

> The earth is the Lord's, and everything in it. The world and all its people belong to Him. For He laid the earth's foundation on the seas and Built it on the ocean depths. Psalm 24:1–2

One of my favorite hymns, "How Great Thou Art" also tells us about the beauty of God's creation.

HOW GREAT THOU ART

O Lord my God, when I in awesome wonder,
Consider all the worlds Thy hands have made;
I see the stars, I hear the rolling thunder,
Thy power throughout the universe displayed.

Then sings my soul, my Savior God, to Thee,
How great Thou art, how great Thou art.
Then sings my soul, my Savior God, to Thee,
How great Thou art, how great Thou art!

When through the woods and forest glades I wander,
And hear the birds sing sweetly in the trees.
When I look down from lofty mountain grandeur
And see the brook and feel the gentle breeze.

Then sings my soul, my Savior God, to Thee,
How great Thou art, how great Thou art.
Then sings my soul, my Savior God, to Thee,
How great Thou art, how great Thou art!

And when I think, that God, His Son not sparing;
Sent Him to die, I scarce can take it in;
That on the Cross, my burden gladly bearing,
He bled and died to take away my sin.

Then sings my soul, my Savior God, to Thee,
How great Thou art, how great Thou art.
Then sings my soul, my Savior God, to Thee,
How great Thou art, how great Thou art!

When Christ shall come, with shout of acclamation,
And take me home, what joy shall fill my heart
Then I shall bow, in humble adoration,
And then proclaim: "My God, how great Thou art!"

Then sings my soul, my Savior God, to Thee,
How great Thou art, how great Thou art.
Then sings my soul, My Savior God, to Thee,
How great Thou art, how great Thou art!

I remember walking through the woods recently and singing "How Great Thou Art." What a wonderful inspirational song! It declares the love of God and the gift of creation! Yes, we have been given the responsibility of overseeing our wonderful environment. So how are we doing?

We know for a fact that we have not been doing the best job at managing the created order and the precious environment. Vice President Al Gore's Nobel Peace Prize winning documentary *An Inconvenient Truth* drives this point home poignantly.

Former Vice President Al Gore shares his concerns on the pressing issue of global warming in this documentary. A long-time environmental activist, Gore first became aware of global warming in the 1970s, and since leaving public office, he has become a passionate advocate for large- and small-scale changes in our laws and lifestyles that could help alleviate this crisis. *An Inconvenient Truth* records a multimedia presentation hosted by Gore, in which he discusses the scientific facts behind global warming, explains its impact on the environment, talks about the disastrous consequences if the world's governments and citizens do not act, and shares what each individual can do to help protect the earth.

According to some projections on rising ocean levels, I might be snorkeling in my living room here in Jupiter, Florida, in less than half a century. My home is located less than a mile from the beach and even closer to the Intercoastal Waterway! Get out the snorkeling gear! That is a very inconvenient truth!

Former Vice President Gore's documentary underscores the importance of thinking and acting locally and globally on the environment. Just as we have a global economy, we also have a global environment. We live on spaceship earth, and each of us has a responsibility to be excellent stewards of the environment which God created. This problem of global warming grew significantly in the last half of the twentieth century.

I grew up in the state of Indiana, one of the Rust Belt states. At one time it was said that the city of Gary, Indiana, was the most polluted town in America. Because of the pollution from the steel mills, the snow fall was not white but whitish red. The air reeked of the smoke that billowed from the steel mills perched on the Lake Michigan shoreline. Air and water pollution were rampant! Since those days, the mills have been under tighter government control, but pollution continues to be an issue.

The same can be said for most of the Rust Belt. The Rust Belt was the economic region in the northeastern quadrant of the United States, located mainly in the midwestern states of Illinois, Indiana, Michigan, and Ohio, as well as Pennsylvania. The term *Rust Belt* gained wide use in the 1970s as the formerly dominant industrial region became noted for the abandonment of factories, unemployment, outmigration, the loss of electoral votes, and overall decline. Since the 1960s, manufacturing cities throughout the Great Lakes region and in the Northeast have suffered a decline in population and economic strength as manufacturers relocated, primarily to the Sun Belt (where I live now!), overseas, or, more recently, to Mexico. Meanwhile, the nation has shifted toward a service economy. Detroit, one of the world's largest manufacturing centers, has been especially hard hit and unable to reduce its dependence on the manufacturing sector. The decline of cities, such as St. Louis, Cleveland, and Akron, Ohio, resulted in dramatic suburban flight. By the 1980s, the economy of some Rust Belt cities had noticeably improved after the introduction or expansion of nonmanufacturing industries. Pittsburgh, initially devastated by cutbacks in its steel industry as early as the late 1950s, has since emphasized its role as a center for research, development, and finance (*The Columbia Electronic Encyclopedia*, 2007).

The reality is that we didn't really think about the environment during the heyday of the industrial revolution. In fact, I remember when the Great Lake Erie was declared dead! William Ashworth writes about it in his book, *The Late, Great Lakes*.

> In the 1960s Lake Erie was declared *dead*, though, ironically, it was full of life—just not the right kind. Eutrophication had claimed Lake Erie and excessive algae became its dominant plant species, covering beaches in slimy moss and killing off

native aquatic species by soaking up all of the oxygen. The demise of Lake Erie is the shallowest and warmest of the five Great Lakes, and the basin is also intensively developed with agriculture, urban areas, industries and sewage treatment plants. For decades, pollution filled Lake Erie with far more nutrients than the lake could handle, with phosphorous being the main culprit.

Phosphorous is a fertilizer that induces plant growth and algae, and it was also found in many commercial detergents at the time. Plants began growing, dying, and decomposing in Lake Erie, creating anoxia (severe deficiency of oxygen) at the bottom of the lake and leaving the water's surface putrid and mossy. The lack of oxygen killed fish and other aquatic species, and the smelly surface repelled anglers, tourists and those living around Lake Erie. Heavy metals also had contaminated much of the fish population of Lake Erie.

In response to public concern and recommendations by the International Joint Commission, the Great Lakes Water Quality Agreement (GLQWA) was signed by the United States and Canada in 1972. The Agreement emphasized the reduction of phosphorous entering lakes Erie and Ontario, and in 1977 maximum levels for phosphorous were added to the Agreement. Also, phosphorus in detergents was finally banned. Coupled with the United States and Canadian Clean Water acts, the GLQWA did much to reduce the phosphorus levels in Lake Erie.

Today, phosphorus loads in Lake Erie are now below the maximum allowed in the GLWQA, and eutrophication has been controlled. Algae and excessive plant growth has been reduced, and native plants are once again growing in sections of the lake. Lake Erie still has many problems— such as non-native invasive species, contaminated sediments and closure of beaches due to sewage contamination. But, through international cooperation and public advocacy, the lake is no longer considered "dead," and, hopefully, people have a better understanding and concern for the effects of human activity on water quality in the Great Lakes and beyond.

The factories had dumped so much pollution into the rivers and the lake that they created an environmental nightmare! It took many years for environmentalists and scientist to bring the lake back to life. The pollution occurred because people were focused on a booming post–World War II economy. Families, businesses, manufacturing, church attendance, baby booming . . . everything was exploding and no one thought much about all of the growth hurting the environment until about the mid-1960s.

That was when we started seeing television commercials telling us not to be litter bugs. What was a litter bug? It was someone driving down the highway and throwing litter out the window. That was a litter bug! No one thought anything about it until the television commercials started making us more aware of the environment. Signs along highways announcing $100 fines for littering really got our attention.

But littering continues to be a huge environmental problem. Many states and countries have initiated campaigns against it. But what can we do about it?

Simple . . . don't litter. It is a spiritual issue!

When we litter we clutter and damage God's earth.

We can also recycle. At first recycling had to be done at the home and transported to recycling centers. Now, many communities around the nation have small recycling bins at individual homes that get picked up each week curbside. This approach is much simpler and easier to enact. Yet I am surprised how many of us still don't recycle. It is a simple discipline that, when enacted, can make a huge impact. For instance, listed below are fun facts about the power of recycling discovered through a simple Google search.

METALS

Recycling one aluminum can saves enough energy—the equivalent of half a gallon of gasoline—to run a TV for three hours.

- 350,000 aluminum cans are produced every minute!
- More aluminum goes into beverage cans than any other product.
- Once an aluminum can is recycled, it can be part of a new can within six weeks.
- Because so many of them are recycled, aluminum cans account for less than 1 percent of the total United States' waste stream, according to the Environmental Protection Agency (EPA) estimates.
- During the time it takes you to read this sentence, 50,000 twelve-ounce aluminum cans are made.
- An aluminum can that is thrown away will still be a can 500 years from now!
- There is no limit to how many times aluminum cans can be recycled.
- Aluminum-can manufacturers have been making cans lighter— in 1972 each pound of aluminum produced 22 cans; today it yields 29 cans.
- We use over 80,000,000,000 aluminum pop cans every year.
- At one time, aluminum was more valuable than gold!
- A 60-watt light bulb can be run for over a day on the amount of energy saved by recycling 1 pound of steel. In one year in the United States, the recycling of steel saves enough energy to heat and light 18,000,000 homes!
- Every ton of recycled steel saves 2,500 pounds of iron ore, 1,000 of coal, and 40 pounds of limestone.

PAPER

To produce each week's Sunday newspapers, 500,000 trees must be cut down.

- Recycling a single run of the Sunday *New York Times* would save 75,000 trees.
- If all our newspapers were recycled, we could save about 250,000,000 trees each year!

- If every American recycled just one-tenth of his or her newspapers, we would save about 25,000,000 trees a year.
- During World War II when raw materials were scarce, 33 percent of all paper was recycled. After the war, this number decreased sharply.
- A 15-year-old tree yields 700 paper grocery bags. A supermarket could use all of them in under an hour! This means in one year, one supermarket goes through 60,500,000 paper bags! Imagine how many supermarkets there are in the U.S.!
- The average American uses seven trees a year in paper, wood, and other wood products. This amounts to about 2,000,000,000 trees per year!
- The amount of wood and paper thrown away each year is enough to heat 50,000,000 homes for 20 years.
- The smell in a dump is the result of paper!
- Approximately one billion trees worth of paper are thrown away every year in the United States.
- Americans use 85,000,000 tons of paper a year, which translates to about 680 pounds per person.
- The average household throws away 13,000 separate pieces of paper each year. Most is packaging and junk mail.
- In 1993, United States paper recovery saved more than 90,000,000 cubic yards of landfill space.
- In 1993 the United States recycled nearly 36,000,000 tons of paper—twice as much as in 1980.
- 27 percent of the newspapers produced in America are recycled.
- Each ton (2000 pounds) of recycled paper can save 17 trees, 380 gallons of oil, three cubic yards of landfill space, 4000 kilowatts of energy, and 7000 gallons of water. This represents 64 percent in energy savings, 58 percent in water savings, and 60 pounds less of air pollution!
- The 17 trees saved (above) can absorb a total of 250 pounds of carbon dioxide from the air each year. Burning that same ton of paper would *create* 1500 pounds of carbon dioxide.

- The construction costs of a paper mill designed to use waste paper is 50 to 80 percent less than the cost of a mill using new pulp.

PLASTIC

Americans use 2,500,000 plastic bottles every hour! Most of them are thrown away!

- Plastic bags and other plastic garbage thrown into the ocean kill as many as 1,000,000 sea creatures every year!
- Americans throw away 25,000,000 plastic beverage bottles every hour!
- Recycling plastic saves twice as much energy as incinerating it.
- Americans throw away 25,000,000,000 Styrofoam coffee cups every year.

GLASS

Every month, we throw out enough glass bottles and jars to fill up a giant skyscraper. All of these jars are recyclable!

- The energy saved from recycling one glass bottle can run a 100-watt light bulb for four hours. It also causes 20 percent less air pollution and 50 percent less water pollution than when a new bottle is made from raw materials.
- A modern glass bottle would take 4000 years or more to decompose—and even longer if it's in the landfill.
- Mining and transporting raw materials for glass produces about 385 pounds of waste for every ton of glass that is made. If recycled glass is substituted for half of the raw materials, the waste is cut by more than 80 percent.

TRASH/LANDFILLS

Although 75 percent of our trash can be recycled, the EPA set a national goal of 25 percent for 1992.

- The first real recycling program was introduced in New York City in the 1890s. The city's first recycling plant was built in 1898.

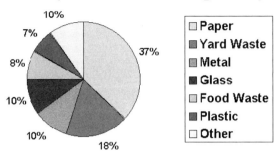

Compositon Of An Average Dump

- Paper 37%
- Yard Waste 18%
- Metal 10%
- Glass 10%
- Food Waste 8%
- Plastic 7%
- Other 10%

- The chart above shows the composition of an average garbage dump. Notice how much of it is recyclable!
- By 1924, 83 percent of American cities were separating some trash items to be reused.
- About one-third of an average dump is made up of packaging material!
- Every year, each American throws out about 1,200 pounds of organic garbage that can be composted.
- New Jersey has the highest recycling rate of all the states: 56 percent!
- The United States is the number one trash-producing country in the world, at 1,609 pounds per person per year. This means that 5 percent of the world's people generate 40 percent of its waste.
- The highest point in Ohio is "Mount Rumpke," which is actually a mountain of trash at the Rumpke sanitary landfill!
- The United States population discards each year 16,000,000,000 diapers, 1,600,000,000 pens, 2,000,000,000 razor blades, 220,000,000 car tires, and enough aluminum to rebuild the United States commercial air fleet four times over.
- Speaking of diapers, a cloth diaper washed at home costs 3 cents per use. A disposable diaper costs 22 cents per use. The difference can add up; a typical baby will use about 10,000 diapers!
- Between 5 and 15 percent of what we throw away contains hazardous substances.

- Out of ever ten dollars spent buying things, one dollar (10 percent) goes toward disposable packaging. Packaging represents about 65 percent of household trash.
- On average, it costs $30 per ton to recycle trash, $50 to send it to the landfill, and $65 to $75 to incinerate it.
- Americans generate and throw away nine times as much waste as Africans or Central Americans, but we also generate two to three times the amount of waste than people living in industrial countries with a comparable or better standard of living do.

MISCELLANEOUS

- More than 20,000,000 Hershey's Kisses are wrapped each day, using 133 square miles of tinfoil. All that foil is recyclable, but not many people realize it.
- Every week about 20 species of plants and animals become extinct!
- McDonald's saves 68,000,000 pounds of packaging per year just by pumping soft drink syrup directly from the delivery truck into tanks in the restaurant, instead of shipping the syrup in cardboard boxes!
- The largest environmental organization in the world is the National Wildlife Federation. It has 5,600,000 members!
- Rainforests are being cut down at the rate of 100 acres per minute!
- One-third of the water used in most homes is flushed down the toilet.
- A single quart of motor oil, if disposed of improperly, can contaminate up to 2,000,000 gallons of fresh water.
- You can walk 1 mile along an average highway in the United States and see about 1,457 pieces of litter.
- The Institute for Local Self-Reliance based in Washington, D.C., calculates that recycling creates 36 jobs per 10,000 tons of material recycled, compared to 6 jobs for every 10,000 of tons brought to traditional disposal facilities.
- A typical family consumes 182 gallons of pop, 29 gallons of juice, 104 gallons of milk, and 26 gallons of bottled water a year. That's a lot of containers—make sure they're recycled!

So how can we Do Greater Things environmentally? One way is to simply recycle and not to litter. That means faith communities across America, every single one of them, could coach their members and constituents to recycle. Each faith community can do greater things environmentally by recycling. Further, it means that the members of the congregation can talk to various people (like business leaders) and institutions (like schools, social organizations, or country clubs) about implementing healthy environmental practices, such as recycling and energy conservation.

All of these approaches are reactionary, but we should also consider proactive approaches. I was traveling to Milwaukee, Wisconsin, in mid-October recently to attend a gathering of friends and colleagues. The plane ride from Cincinnati to Milwaukee looked to be rather quiet until my seat mate took the window seat. We began talking, and he told me that he worked for a company that made automobile batteries. The more we talked, the more I realized that this gentleman was committed to the research and development of batteries for hybrid vehicles. He was a committed environmentalist. He told me that if we could create hybrid vehicles that traveled long distances that we would not have to be oil dependant. Then he pointed me to the Rocky Mountain Institute where he had spoken at a conference on going green with the automobile.

I went to their Web site and discovered that the Rocky Mountain Institute is committed to creating a healthy, viable environment. These two paragraphs from their Web site (www.rmi.org) illustrate that point quite well:

Rocky Mountain Institute (RMI) is a organization that fosters the efficient and restorative use of resources so that companies, governments and organizations are more efficient, make more money, and do less harm to the environment. RMI is engaged in cutting-edge research on oil independence, renewable energy technologies, distributed energy, resource planning, green buildings, and radically efficient transportation.

Our innovations have profoundly influenced the energy sector, helped corporations to change how they do business, and informed governments about key enabling policy reforms. RMI areas of expertise include: energy use and supply, buildings & land development, transportation, manufacturing, climate protection, and community economic development.

Now that's proactive! Doing Greater Things Environmentally proactively looks not only at what we can do as individuals, but how we can influence others to do something greater for the environment.

I am looking for Do Greater Things Environmental champions. If you are one or know of someone or an organization who is a champion, please write to me. I want to hear your story and perhaps share it through our Web site and other Greater Things Enterprises communication tools.

POINTS TO PONDER

- The environment is going to be an increasingly important issue.
- God made us stewards over our environment.
- It is not local; it is global and local. You can make a difference.
- The whole world is integrated, interrelated, and interlinked in every way.
- Don't litter. It is a spiritual issue!
- Doing Greater Things Environmentally proactively looks not only at what we can do as individuals, but how we can influence others to do something greater for the environment.

QUESTIONS FOR REFLECTION

- Do I currently recycle? If not, why not?
- If so, how can I encourage others in my circle of influence to do the same?
- What can I do to create an awareness in my own spirit, as well as that of the spirit of others, in terms of the environment?

CHAPTER 14

DO GREATER THINGS BY LEAVING A LASTING LEGACY

I want to talk to you about the meaning of success, significance, and leaving a lasting legacy as we strive to do greater things. What is success? It is:

1. The favorable or prosperous conclusion of attempts or endeavors.
2. The attainment of wealth, position, honors, or such like.
3. A successful performance or achievement.
4. A person or thing that is successful.

What is significance?

Significance:
1. Importance; consequence
2. Meaning; import
3. The quality of being significant or meaningful

What is a legacy? It is:
1. (In a will) a gift of property, especially personal property, as money; bequest.

2. Anything handed down from the past, as from an ancestor or predecessor.
3. The office, function, or commission of a legate.

Success! Significance! Legacy! These three words, when combined, reflect a Greater Things faith style that leads to Greater Things lifestyle. Expecting Greater Things is about how to be in a relationship with God, ourselves, and others. Growing in Greater Things is about how to experience significance spiritually, relationally, and financially. Doing Greater Things is all about creating a legacy in your community and the environment through your generosity; it is about leaving a long-lasting legacy after your last breath. The good news is that our last breath on earth is marked by a comma, not a period, when we live as people of faith. We move from strength in this life to strength in life eternal. That is exciting!

The Bible teaches us that our success and significance are not born in a vacuum. Rather, it is inherited from those who have come before us. In fact, the Bible teaches us there is more to it than a lasting legacy. People of faith who have died live in God for all eternity. Consequently, they leave us a lasting and living legacy.

In fact, the writer of the New Testament book of Hebrews tells that we actually are surrounded by a great cloud of witnesses who experienced success, significance, and the power of a lasting and living legacy. The author tells us of faithful people of old, such as Abraham, Jacob, and Joshua, just to name a few.

Abraham framed his life and the life of his family so that all of their success, joy, comfort, and prosperity were deeply rooted in a strong faith in God. In fact, God gave Abraham a legacy that said all the people of the world were his descendants. Wow! Talk about a lasting legacy.

You see, a lasting legacy can be about leaving behind money and material possessions for others, but it doesn't always have to be so. For instance, when Ida Cromer died, she left behind a lasting legacy because her story of generosity, faith, love, and vision will be told in my family for a very long time. It has been told in this book, and I talk about it in my keynotes, seminars, and workshops. And, with the establishment of the Greater Things Ida Cromer Travel Scholarship, others will benefit from her vision and faith. The ripple effect will touch hundreds, perhaps thousands, of lives! And that will be part of my legacy as well.

Another great story from the Bible is that of Jacob. Jacob was successful, significant, and he left a lasting legacy because he displayed three characteristics for living a Greater Things lifestyle: generosity, zealousness, and industriousness.

Generosity: he had a pleasing personality and a commitment to doing more than expected.

Zealousness: he had a burning passion that was contagious!

Industriousness: he had a mission, a quest. That burning goal implanted by previous experiences drove him to succeed! His energy was turned to synergy.

When these three characteristics are used in service to God and others, the practitioner is truly successful, significant, and leaves a lasting legacy.

Another person from the Bible is Joshua. He was a great leader who was known for fighting the battle of Jericho where the walls came tumbling down. A great military leader and Moses' successor, he experienced victory after victory because he led his people and taught them to fully trust God and obey His commands. They committed their ways to God, and God blessed them abundantly.

The same holds true for us! When we commit our ways to God and follow His teachings, great things happen in our lives. We are amazed at the blessings that come our way.

I experienced this truth while working on this book this past week. First, I met with some people who had been reading an author's copy of the book. I wanted to get their opinion. They loved it. Then they said, "You have a business plan that will help get your ideas and coaching out across the country and around the world. We want to help make that happen!" Wow! It's because of their faith in God and passion for excellence and sharing God's love that the Greater Things Enterprises business plan is moving from vision to reality. That was the first blessing.

The second blessing happened yesterday. I called the Crystal Cathedral and spoke with Dr. Schuller's executive assistant. We had been talking for several weeks about the possibility of Dr. Schuller writing the foreword to this book. She said, "I finally have an answer! He wants to write it and will be happy to do so. This doesn't happen very often. Congratulations, John!" I was ecstatic! I said, "I am so excited and honored to have his help! It's because I expected greater things!" It's true! Exercise your faith and see the amazing greater things that God brings into your life.

This is actually a principle found in the book of Proverbs (16:3): commit to the Lord whatever you do, and your plans will succeed! This principle assumes added significance because it is also echoed in the teaching of Jesus (Mathew 6:33): Seek first the Kingdom of God and His righteousness and all these things shall be added unto you!

You and I can experience success and significance, and we can create a lasting legacy if we follow these two teachings. It's all about keeping the right focus! Where should that focus be placed? The writer of Hebrews tells us . . .

> **12:1** Therefore, since we are surrounded by such a great cloud of witnesses, let us throw off everything that hinders and the sin that so easily entangles, and let us run with perseverance the race marked out for us.
>
> **12:2** Let us fix our eyes on Jesus, the author and perfecter of our faith, who for the joy set before him endured the cross, scorning its shame, and sat down at the right hand of the throne of God.

I love that particular text! It tells us that we live in a continuum of grace, and that we are never alone. It tells us that, as we run this race in life, we are being urged on by all those people of faith who have passed on! They have run the race before us. They are part of that great cloud of witnesses. Consequently, they bring us a lasting, living legacy.

Notice the tense of the text: We *are* surrounded by a great cloud of witnesses, not "We *were* surrounded." What does this look like?

Do Greater Things by Leaving a Lasting Legacy 161

One of the best contemporary pop expressions of the great cloud of witnesses is found in Bill Kean's cartoons in *Family Circus*. I have found three of my favorites to share with you.

The first depicts the saying that the healthy family knows it doesn't live in a continuum. The Bible and modern psychology tell us that the healthy and godly families experience blessings from generation to generation. The caption of the cartoon says, "This will be a portrait of all the men in our family," and it shows those who are alive and those who have died in the faith but live in the great cloud of witnesses.

The second tells us that the great cloud of witnesses teems with life. The cartoon shows little Jeffy asking his mother, "Did I play with Granddad much when I was little?" Mother replies, "No, Dear, he died before you were born." Jeffy replies, as he runs outside to play, "Poor Granddad, he missed out on me!" His grandfather, looking down from heaven with some friends, says, "Hear that, everybody? Another one-liner from ol' Jeffy! What a great grandson!"

I remember the first time I encountered death in my family. My Uncle Harv, a great fix-it man, died when I was five years old. I remember him fixing everything around our house. He was a nice man, and he always let me watch him fix things. When he died, I asked my mother if I would ever see him again. She said, "Yes, someday you will. But better yet, every time you think about Uncle Harv, he lives in your mind and heart." I never forgot that. Then, years later, when I learned about how the great cloud of witnesses cheer us on in running the race of life, Mother's words made even more sense.

My father passed away on November 30, 1982, and it was the same day in 2007 that my mentor in faith, Dr. Schuller, agreed to write the Foreword to this book. I imagined Father watching with delight the man who had helped restore his faith offering to help me share with the world my passion and stories for Expecting Greater Things!

We do not live in a vacuum. We are interconnected, interrelated, and multidimensional. God is with us at all times and encourages us in our lives.

The third cartoon moves from the nuclear family to the family of God. It happens on an Easter Sunday and the church is packed! The choir is singing "Alleluia! Alleluia!" Two children say to one another, "Churches must be the busiest places on earth at Easter." "Well, I hope it's peaceful and quiet for Granddad up in heaven." The scene shifts to heaven. A friend of Granddad asks, "Hear that conversation between two of your grandkids, Al?" He replies, "No, I'm too busy! I'll replay it later." Another person says, "This is always our biggest day. Next is Christmas and Yom Kippur and . . ." Another says, "More prayers just in . . ." Someone else says, "I'm still catching up from all the sunrise services." Still another says, pointing to the church, "There's another face and another face."

Yes, because we have such a great cloud of witnesses, let us run the race and win the prize! Let us live our lives in such a way that we leave a positive, dynamic, and lasting legacy!

But how is this interpersonal relational legacy accomplished? It is achieved through building relationship equity. This is a phrase that I coined at a presentation that I made to several real estate executives, agents, brokers, and attorneys at a conference in Fort Lauderdale some years ago. The sponsor asked me to speak to the significance of ethics, values, and relationships on the bottom line of business.

The more I reflected on the most flourishing times in my life in terms of accomplishments, investments, career, and business, it occurred to me that I had been successful because of the relationship equity that I had built over the years. Each positive, healthy, and dynamic relationship adds equity to my life's path. And, in return, my proactive participation in people's lives adds value to theirs. There's an old saying, "You can never out give God!" That is true. I also believe you can't out give people and life! Norman Vincent Peale wrote:

> The man who lives for himself is a failure. Even if he gains much wealth, position or power, he is still a failure. The man who lives for others has achieved true success. A rich man who concentrates his wealth and position for the good of humanity

is a success. A poor man who gives his service and his sympathy to others has achieved true success, even though material property or outward honors never come to him.

Albert Einstein summed it up this way, "The value of a person should be seen in what that person gives and not in what that person is able to achieve."

Jesus said, "It is better to give than it is to receive" (Acts 20:35). Someone much later added to this sage advice: "Yes, it is better. Besides, you don't have to write thank-you notes."

Seneca, the Roman poet of ancient times, wrote, "No man can live happily who regards himself alone, who turns everything to his own advantage. You must live for others, if you wish to live for yourself."

That is how to build relationship equity. The key is to give as much as you can. In the midst of giving you receive without ever expecting it. This is what it is to experience success, significance, and a lasting legacy.

Within every person there is a dream, a hope, a vision. What is your dream? What is your vision? What are your goals? What kind of legacy do you want to leave?

Woodrow Wilson aid, "You are not here merely to make a living. You are here in order to enable the world to live more amply, with greater vision, with a finer spirit of hope and achievement. You are here to enrich the world, and you impoverish yourself if you forget the errand."

Henry David Thoreau stated, "In the long run, people only hit what they aim at. Therefore, they had better aim at something high."

At what are you aiming? Can you achieve it without the help of God? If you can, then aim higher! Is it still low enough that you can reach it without the help of God, but with the help and support of others? Then aim still higher! Is it still low enough that you can attain it through your powers as well as the power of your friends, family, and associates? Then aim still higher! Expect Greater Things! Ask God for anything and God will provide if it benefits others and brings Him glory! Remember? You will do greater things! Aim high!

One of my visions is to equip individuals, organizations, and businesses with the power and conviction to leave a lasting legacy by expecting, growing, and doing greater things with their lives. I have shared stories about people and organizations that are doing greater things right now! They are making a substantial difference with their lives and living life to the fullest. And it is my hope that their stories inspire you to live a Greater Things lifestyle.

But what about living and planning in such a way that we leave a long-lasting legacy after we are gone? This can happen relationally, spiritually, materially, and financially when we are committed to doing greater things.

We have already explored how this happens relationally (relationship equity) and spiritually (great cloud of witnesses), but how can this happen materially and financially?

Studies predict a transfer of over thirty trillion dollars in wealth over the next twenty years from the greatest generation and the early baby boomers to the later boomers and their children. Studies also show that unless the inheritors learn and apply wealth-management principles (see Grow in Greater Things Financially), the wealth will not last beyond their generation. But if wealth-management principles are learned and applied, more wealth will be created and more charitable giving exercised. In addition, through excellent estate and charitable planning, lasting legacies will be created.

Part of my vision is to equip you with the tools necessary for managing the wealth that you are going to bequeath or inherit. The Greater Things Enterprises Web site will help you advance in this area in terms of education, financial planning, estate planning, and charitable gifting. You will find this under the Grow in Greater Things Wealth Management section of the Web site.

There are so many amazing tools that will help you. Our Greater Things partner companies will coach you on maximizing what you have now. And we will help you create a lasting legacy. After all, if we can properly leverage what God has given us, then we can truly expect, grow, and do greater things.

POINTS TO PONDER

- Success! Significance! Legacy! These three words, when combined, reflect a Greater Things faith-style that leads to a Greater Things lifestyle.
- Doing Greater Things is all about creating a legacy in your community and the environment through your generosity; it is about leaving a long-lasting legacy after your last breath.
- A lasting legacy can be about leaving behind money and material possessions for others, but it doesn't always have to be so.
- Exercise your faith and see the amazing greater things that God brings into your life.
- We do not live in a vacuum. We are interconnected, interrelated, and multidimensional. God is with us at all times and encourages us in our lives.
- Each positive, healthy, and dynamic relationship adds equity to our life's path.

QUESTIONS FOR REFLECTIONS

- At what am I aiming? Can I achieve it without the help of God? If so, then is it truly a greater thing to God's glory and the benefit of others?
- Who has gone on in life before me? What lessons have I learned from them?
- What equity do I have in my life that I can leverage to the glory of God and the building of a healthy, happy life?

CHAPTER 15

EXPECT, GROW, AND DO GREATER THINGS!

> The future belongs to people who see possibilities before they become obvious.
> Theodore Levitt, Harvard Business School

This is true in your personal and spiritual life. It materializes in your family and social life. And it is true in your business and professional life. If you expect greater things, you will learn to see the possibilities! As you grow in greater things, you will be able to develop that potential into reality. Then you will do greater things by leveraging those tangible realities into lasting legacies!

I know these things to be true because they have happened to me time and time again. This book is a document of proof! God has blessed my journey with amazing people and experiences. He has made it possible for me to study ancient, as well as contemporary thinkers and leaders, and benefit from their wisdom. The more I study, learn, and experience, the more I realize that life is an amazing journey filled with Greater Things opportunities for growth, service, and excellence.

You might wonder where I came up with the Greater Things theme and concept. Yes, it was the teaching found in John 14:12–14. You remember:

> I tell you the truth, anyone who has faith in me will do what I have been doing. He will do even greater things than these, because I am going to the Father. And I will do whatever you ask in my name, so that the Son may bring glory to the Father. You may ask me for anything in my name, and I will do it.

That, however, is not the whole story.

I will never forget the experience. It was similar to my call to ministry when I was a teenager, but this time the call was clear and to the point. I was sitting in my home office overlooking the lake in my Granger, Indiana, home on February 20, 1997. I had just finished my time in prayer and was having a cup of coffee at my desk in my new leather-back executive chair. (In fact, I am sitting at the very same desk as I write this paragraph.)

I was praying, writing in my journal, and reading my Bible and a book of quotes. Suddenly, I felt a nudge in my spirit, and I started writing an outline for a vision plan that would be called Greater Things.

Within twenty minutes I had the entire concept for expecting, growing in, and doing greater things to the glory of God. It was a combination of all the work that I had done in Russia from 1992 to 1997, as well as the culmination of my efforts in business, wealth management, investing, and serving as a pastor since the age of nineteen. Further, it was a compilation of what I had learned, both as attendee or leader, at conferences, workshops, keynotes, seminars, and retreats. And it was my deepest desire to take all of this experience, combine it with reason and tradition, as well as my love for the scriptures and ancient teaching, and create a meaningful articulation of God's love, power, and effectiveness. I knew I wanted to reach both the communities of worship, as well as the people of faith who had not yet experienced a healthy worship community.

I also knew that this philosophy of expecting, growing, and doing greater things would have a far-reaching impact as the leaders of business, politics, medicine, education, entertainment, athletics, and faith discovered the power of Greater Things applications for their field of expertise.

I knew that there needed to be a one-stop shop on the web for Expecting, Grow in, and Doing Greater Things. You can see the best listings of books, products, and services from myself and like-minded Greater Things pioneers and champions here. On this site you can advance your spiritual growth, financial savvy, and have the tools for living life to the fullest.

Further, I knew in my heart, mind, and soul that these teachings could be spread by finding like-minded people and lifting them up as Greater Things Champions. I envisioned a television and radio program that would celebrate these champions and broadcast their stories. I envisioned their stories appearing on the Greater Things Web site and in book form. All of these produced materials will be featured on the Expect Greater Things section of the Web site.

My vision expanded to creating financial-planning and wealth-management services that embodied the principles discussed in this book. The vision included identifying like-minded partners who could ethically and effectively create plans to help greater things materialize in people's lives. The implementation of the vision would begin on the Web with referrals, and develop into one-on-one meetings, all of which would be featured on the Grow in Greater Things section of the Web site.

The vision also foresaw the creation of Grow in Greater Things Travel Opportunities with a partner travel company. They would be top-of-the-line trips for Greater Things Participants, featuring an online study curriculum prior to the trip. These travel adventures throughout the world, besides providing wonderful experiences, would feature Greater Things Champions as keynote speakers. Some of these travels would include the opportunity to do greater things by serving the needy. These trips would be featured on the Grow in Greater Things section of our Web site.

My vision included identifying healthy faith communities where faith could grow through active fellowship and applied service at the local level. The same could be true in the area of community service. These would be found in the Do Greater Things section of the Web site.

The Do Greater Things section of the Web site will feature our Greater Things champions' favorite charities and philanthropic organizations. I want to inform you about the wonderful opportunities to contribute your time, talent, and resources to help others.

And my vision included creating a nonprofit Greater Things Institute that would promote new concepts as they developed for Doing Greater Things—the Ida Cromer Greater Things Travel Scholarship being the first. You will be able to contribute to this scholarship so that others in various disciplines who embody a vision for greater things can be supported in their growth! The Greater Things Institute will start with this pilot project and, through faith and action, other projects will be added.

This all happened in twenty minutes on February 20, 1997. The vision was like an amazing download from God. And, like my first calling, it would not let me go! My life was forever changed on that day so that your life perhaps could be impacted as you expected greater things to fulfill your God-given potential as a person of faith.

Following this experience, I explored every avenue to make the vision a reality. In fact, I developed and followed the pattern that I shared earlier in this book:

THE PROCESS OF VISION . . .

Starts with a heart in prayer
Evaluates resources under one's care
And studies from there
Then networks and shares
And it is owned by those who care
Then it is broadcast from there

The vision started with a heart in prayer at my desk on February 20, 1997.

When I evaluated my resources, I realized the vision was so big that I needed help from others. So I began to identify partners who could help me make the vision a reality. I also realized that the vision was going to be much more expensive than I could afford.

Next I networked with trusted friends, relatives, and associates. Everyone said, "Great vision! Keep at it." But most people are busy with their own lives. I learned that sometimes you have to be the sole keeper of your vision, and that patience in that regard is not only a virtue—it is a requirement!

Then I found out that a vision is owned by those who care and believe in it. In 1999 I spent one to two weeks every month for almost ten months traveling to Newport Beach, California. Mark and Cherilyn Moehlman shared my vision, and they extended their Southern California hospitality by inviting me into their lovely home. Mark and I networked! Then we networked. And we networked some more. We worked with some wonderful attorneys and even created a private placement memorandum so that the company could be staffed and funded. We were all ready to go when the dot com bust blew! The economy stalled and so did the vision. I was shell-shocked and disillusioned. I remember saying to God, "Why did you give me this vision? It isn't working!"

God has three answers to prayer: yes, no, and wait! God's answer obviously was "Wait." And, now, eight years later, the vision is being broadcast through this book and the Greater Things Enterprises Web site: www.expectgreaterthings.com.

I found myself wondering why this vision was taking so long to realize. I found myself speaking about it, writing articles about it, studying, and keynoting across the nation. What I didn't realize was that God and life were shaping the vision in me and making it a reality in the way I lived. I stayed focused!

The most telling experience occurred during my trip to Greece and Turkey in 1998. I had led a group of sixteen people from my congregation in Indiana on a trip. We visited the island of Patmos where John had written the New Testament book of Revelation.

He was imprisoned in a cave with one entrance that led down a flight of stairs fifty feet below ground. Our group descended the rock-hewn staircase, and we listened to our guide describe John's imprisonment and writing.

A gentle breeze apparently came from nowhere because the only opening to the cave was the doorway fifty feet above us. Ah, but the breeze came from somewhere, from someone. We all felt it; it brought us peace. As the breeze washed over my body, I heard a small voice say, "Write." I said, "What shall I write?" And the Spirit said, "Write."

So, now after nine years, I will write. To God be the glory!

Some closing Greater Things thoughts . . .

It is my hope that you are inspired and ready to set out on an adventure! It is my prayer that you are ready to celebrate being a Greater Things champion!

Join me on this journey. Visit our Web site, and let's see the power of faith in action.

> ### POINTS TO PONDER
> - If you expect greater things, you will learn to see the possibilities!
> - As you grow in greater things, you will develop that potential into reality.
> - You will do greater things by leveraging those realities into lasting legacies!
>
> ### QUESTIONS FOR REFLECTION
> - Why is God calling me to expect greater things today?
> - Why do I believe that God is passionate about me growing in greater things oday?
> - Why do I know that I am supposed to do greater things with my life today?

EPILOGUE

It is my honor to walk with you in the journey for Expecting, Growing and Doing Greater Things. This is just the first step in the journey. Over the next several years we will walk together and discover God's amazing journey for us, our nation and our world. But, it begins with the first step . . . .

Please send me your stories about Expecting . . . Growing . . . Doing Greater Things.

Tell me about your experiences.

And, by all means, tell me stories of Greater Things Champions.

We all are interconnected. We are all part of a continuum. We all have an equal story to share, no matter where we come from or where we are right now at this very second.

God is good . . . all the time. He wants us to achieve greater things to His glory and for the betterment of all people.

Expect!

Grow!

Do!

Greater Things.

AN INVITATION FROM THE AUTHOR TO CONTINUE THE GREATER THINGS JOURNEY

Look for my next two books to be released soon. They will build upon the Greater Things theme! Here is what you can expect.

Twelve Greater Things Principles For Excellence in Living

Want to maximize your God-given potential? broaden your sphere of influence to serve others? unleash, increase, and inspire the best there is in yourself and others? You can achieve all of this by eliminating the negative and instilling the following Twelve Greater Things Principles. These penetrating principles are:

- The Power of Vision
- Passion for Excellence
- Compassion for People
- Determination to Redefine the Circle
- Commitment to Serving Others Locally and Globally
- Commitment to Excellence in Leadership
- Willingness to Embrace Change for the Sake of the Mission

Passion for Living by the "Five P's": Prayer, Purpose, People, Program, Property

The Importance of Sharing the Load

Willingness to Be an Excellent Steward

Willingness to Exhaust Every Possible Means

The Desire to Glorify God

As you can see, these principles build on the Greater Things theme. They come from years of experience and study. They will impact your life in meaningful and significant ways!

The second book is the Professional Edition for Congregational Leaders, wherein the principles of the first book are applied to congregations.

Dr. John R. Myers
March 1, 2008
drjohnrmyers@yahoo.com
www.expectgreaterthings.com

SELECT BIBLIOGRAPHY

An Inconvenient Truth. DVD. Directed by Davis Guggenheim. 2006; Hollywood: Paramount.

Ashworth, William. *The Late, Great Lakes: An Environmental History (Great Lakes Books)*. Detroit: Wayne State University Press, 1987.

Bechard, Raymond. *Unspeakable: The Hidden Truth Behind The World's Fastest Growing Crime*. New York: Compel Publishing, 2006.

Boberg, Carl G., and R. J. Hughes. *United Methodist Hymnal: Book of United Methodist Worship*. "How Great Thou Art." Nashville: United Methodist Publishing House, 1989: 77.

Bonhoeffer, Dietrich. *The Cost of Discipleship*. London: Macmillian Publishing Co., 1969.

Bradbury, William, and Charlotte Elliott. *United Methodist Hymnal: Book of United Methodist Worship*. "Just As I Am." Nashville: United Methodist Publishing House, 1989: 357.

Caddyshack 2. DVD. Directed by Allan Arkush. 1988; Burbank: Warner Home Video.

Chesterton, G. K. *Chesterton Day by Day: The Wit and Wisdom of G. K. Chesterton*. Seattle, WA: Inkling Books, 2002.

"Code of Hammurabi @ Gavel2Gavel.com. Summary and Full Text." Online library of internet and reference resources. http://www.re-quest.net/g2g/historical/laws/hammurabi/index.htm (accessed January 15, 2008).

Forrest Gump. DVD. Directed by Robert Zemeckis. 1994; Hollywood: Paramount.

Foster, Richard J.. *Money Sex and Power Study Guide*. New York: Harperone, 1985.

Guest, John. *Finding Deeper Intimacy With God: Only a Prayer Away*. Grand Rapids: Baker Pub Group, 1992.

Guillen, Dr. Michael . "Lovestruck." The Rethink Conference, The Crystal Cthedral, Garden Grove, January 17, 2008.

Hill, Napoleon. *Think and Grow Rich!: The Original Version, Restored and Revised*. San Diego, CA: Aventine Press, 2004.

Holy Bible: The New King James Version (Pew Library Edition). Waco, TX: Thomas Nelson, 1994.

It's a Wonderful Life. DVD. Directed by Frank Capra. 1946; Hollywood: Paramount.

Keane, Bil. *Count Your Blessings: A Family Circus Collection*. Colorado Springs, CO: Focus on the family Publishing, 1995.

Lagasse, Paul. *Columbia Encyclopedia Sixth Edition*. Los Angles: Columbia, 1993

Morris, Gary. *True Wealth: Reflections On What Matters Most In Life (Blue Mountain Arts Collection)*. Finley, OH: Blue Mountain Press, 2004.

Morris, Holly J. "Happiness Explained: New science shows how to inject real joy into your life." *U.S. News and World Report*, August 26, 2001: 46-54.

New International Version. Colorado Springs: International Bible Society, 1978.

New Revised Standard Version. Grand Rapids: Zondervan, 1990.

"Rocky Mountain Institute : Abundance By Design." Rocky Mountain Institute : Abundance By Design. http://www.rmi.org (accessed January 15, 2008).

Schweitzer, Albert. *Memoirs of Childhood and Youth.* London: George Allen & Unwin, 1924.

Stream, Carol. *Connection Newsletter*. ChristianityToday.com. Illinois: September 8, 2004.

Williams, Margery. *The Velveteen Rabbit*. Boston: Avon, 1999.

USA Today. November 23, 1999. "Research by Yankelovich Partners for the Lutheran Brotherhood."

InfoCision

Good	Bad
paid every monday.	only $9/hr
	split days off
	2nd shift
	No time for fun life or projects
	3 hrs btwn brks
	might not get 40 hrs